CW01636121

أربعون حديثا في الأخلاق

43 Prophetic Narrations on Developing the Character & Reforming the Soul with Commentary

Compiled by
Mufti Abdussamad Ahmed

Commentary by
Muawiyah ibn Mufti Abdussamad Ahmed

ZAINAB AWAN

All rights reserved. No part of this publication may be reproduced, stored in a retrieval system, or transmitted in any form by means of electronic, mechanical, photocopying or otherwise, without the prior permission of the distributors.

British Library Cataloguing in Publication Data
A catalogue record for this book is available from the British Library.

Published & Distributed by:

Jamiatul Ilm Wal Huda
30 Moss Street
Blackburn
Lancashire, U.K.
BB1 5JT
T: 01254 673105
W: www.jamiah.co.uk
E: info@jamiah.co.uk

Compiled by: Mufti Abdussamad Ahmed
Commentary by: Muawiyah ibn Mufti Abdussamad Ahmed
E: muawiyahahmed@hotmail.co.uk

Edited by: Amir Isap

ISBN: **978-1-910967-06-5**

Printed by: **Imak Ofset**, **Turkey**

بسم الله الرحمن الرحيم

In the name of Allah, the most Merciful, the ever Kind

قال النبيّ صلّى الله عليه وسلّم:

"مَا مِنْ شَيْءٍ أَثْقَلُ فِيْ الْمِيْزَانِ مِنْ حُسْنِ الْخُلُقِ" (سنن أبي داود)

The Prophet Muhammad PBUH mentioned:

Nothing is weightier in the scale of a believer than good character

(Sunan Abu Dawood)

Introduction

In the name of Allah, the most Merciful, the ever Kind. All praise belongs to Allah, Lord of the universe and Master of our fortunes, may peace and blessings be showered upon our beloved Prophet Muhammad ﷺ, his companions and upon all who follow in their footsteps.

Islam is a complete religion. The rulings of Islam are not restricted to mere acts of worship to Almighty Allah. Rather, the holistic nature of the religion includes guidance that ranges from interactions with our fellow human beings, animals and even the environment to the building of human civilisation. The science of akhlaaq includes inculcating good character, personal development of the self and reformation of the soul. No doubt, they form key aspects in the lives of believers. A cursory glance at a few of the proverbs from the Holy Qur'an, authentic prophetic narrations and pearls from the pious predecessors will accurately provide a barometer into appreciating the importance of developing the character and reforming the soul.

Almighty Allah mentions in regard to the Prophet Muhammad ﷺ, 'And indeed, you (O Muhammad) are of a great moral character'. [Al-Qalam, 68:4]

Prophet Muhammad ﷺ mentioned, 'Nothing is weightier in the scale of the believer on the day of judgment than good character'. [Sunan Abu Dawood, 4799]

Prophet Muhammad ﷺ mentioned, 'Indeed a believer can reach the ranks of the one who fasts throughout the day and stands in night prayer by merely adopting good character'. [Sunan Abu Dawood, 4798]

In fact, the Prophet Muhammad ﷺ once mentioned, 'Good character... increases the life of an individual (and is a means of blessings)'. [Musnad Ahmad, 25259]

The life of the Prophet Muhammad ﷺ is filled with numerous examples that portray exemplary character, from amongst them is the incident of the Bedouin who urinated in the mosque. The companions were ready to pounce on the Bedouin and rebuke him harshly for urinating in the sanctified area. However, the Prophet Muhammad ﷺ held them back and instructed them to be calm and collected in their reaction. He taught them to treat him with love and compassion and whilst maintaining his composure, he instructed them to wash away the urine. He then uttered the words, 'Indeed, you have been sent as people who facilitate ease and not as those who create difficulty'. [Saheeh al-Bukhari, 6128]

The renowned scholar, Ibrahim ibn Habeeb ibn ash-Shaheed once advised his son thus; 'O son, go to the jurists and scholars and seek knowledge from them. Take from them their manners and their wisdom, for that is more beloved to me than you compiling a great number of Prophetic Narrations'. [al-Jami' of al-Khateeb al-Baghdadi, 1/80]

Imam ibn al-Qayyim mentioned, 'Religion is good character, whoever increases in good character has indeed increased in religion'. [Madarij as-Salikeen of Ibn al-Qayyim, 2/307]

Hafidh ibn Rajab al-Hanbali mentioned, '*Taqwa* (God consciousness) cannot be attained except with the adorning of oneself with good character'. [Jami' al-'Uloom wal-Hikam, 18]

The scholar, 'Abdurrahman al-Maydani has divided good character into four categories; interactions between the human being and the Creator, interactions between human beings with other humans, the interactions of an individual in regard to themselves, the interactions between the human being and non-humans. He then goes on to provide examples of each and indicates that the rights of the four different categories are mandatory to fulfil. He clarifies that it is possible for people to adorn themselves with such beautiful character that they fulfil that which is from the rights of Almighty Allah whilst simultaneously fulfilling the rights due towards oneself, other human beings and non-humans too. [al-Akhlaaq al-Islaamiyyah of 'Abdurrahman al-Maydani, 1/52]

The Prophet Muhammad ﷺ would consistently supplicate to Almighty Allah with, 'O Allah, guide me to the best of character, for indeed, nobody guides to the best of character except Yourself. O Allah, protect me from evil character, for nobody can remove bad character except Yourself'. [Saheeh Muslim, 1848]

The few statements above clearly indicate towards the emphasis Islam lays on upholding good character and removing the vices and bad character from our lives. Hence, the aim of this compilation was to present 43 Prophet Narrations in regard to matters pertaining to developing the character. This ranges from the rectification of the intentions and worshiping Almighty Allah to helping the community (Muslim or non-Muslim) and even caring for animals. This includes all facets of society; showing respect and reverence to the scholars and the elderly to displaying compassion towards the young. All of which have been discussed at length in light of the Quranic verses, authentic Prophetic Narrations and wisdoms from the pious scholars. The length of explanation adopted is of a consistent nature for each narration; neither a very lengthy explanation which could bore the reader, nor a very brief explanation which may result in ambiguity in understanding the texts. Furthermore, the length and choice of words is specifically chosen to facilitate teachers to use the book to deliver lessons, for scholars to employ in their lectures and speeches and for parents to use as short daily or even weekly study-circles in the homes. May Almighty Allah allow us all to take immense benefit from this book, the teachings of the Holy Qur'an, the Prophetic narrations and the wisdoms of the pious scholars.

For the completion of this compilation, I must express my gratitude and show an immense appreciation to many. First and foremost, I would like to thank the Creator, Almighty Allah, for granting me the ability to understand, comprehend and express the teachings of the Holy Qur'an, the Prophetic narrations and the wisdoms of the pious scholars. There is no doubt, without this blessing of the Almighty Allah, one would be incapable of completing the most minute of tasks. Furthermore, I would like to thank all the people who helped in the compilation of this work and I pray Almighty Allah makes this work a means of entry into Paradise without any reckoning for all of us. I want to express a special gratitude to my dear father and respected teacher, Mufti Abdussamad Ahmed. His teachings, spiritual upbringing, advice and guidance have always been instrumental for me in all my endeavours. I am grateful to him for selecting 43 beautiful Prophetic narrations relating to the science of *akhlaaq*. I also want to extend a special thanks to my dear friend Amir Isap who did a thorough edit of the whole book repeatedly, ensuring the book is an easy-read for the scholarly and laity alike. I pray Almighty Allah increase him and all others in knowledge and adorn us all with the best of character; the character of Prophet Muhammad ﷺ.

May Almighty Allah make the work a means of great success for all of us in both worlds, especially the ultimate success of entering Paradise without reckoning and gaining the pleasure of Almighty Allah. Aameen.

Muawiyah ibn Mufti Abdussamad Ahmed

إِنَّمَا الْأَعْمَالُ بِالنِّيَّاتِ

Verily, actions are (rewarded) in accordance to the intentions

(Sahih al-Bukhari)

This narration emphasises the importance of intentions, prior to the undertaking of any action; even if it be a day-to-day task, an individual should rectify and correct their intention, as this renders the action into one that gathers and accumulates reward.

If an individual performs an action without any intention, then they will not receive reward for that action, however, the mere formulation of a correct intention prior to that action can be the means of immense reward.

For example, if an individual sits to eat without making an intention, then they will neither be sinful for it, nor will they be rewarded for it. Nevertheless, if an individual sits to eat with the intention that they will perform virtuous and righteous deeds by means of the energy gained from this food, then this action of eating will become rewarding.

A further example is of the individual who dons a watch, if void of any intention, then neither will they acquire any reward, nor any sin. However, if an individual dons a watch with the intention that he will be able to use it as a means to assist him in becoming punctual (with his prayers etc.), then this wearing of the watch will becoming a means of gathering reward.

This narration of 'actions are in accordance to the intentions' is regarded as a primary narration amongst the scholars and is regarded as a very important narration, indicating to its importance. Imam Ahmad ibn Hanbal RA would indicate towards three narrations as being from amongst the foundations and roots of Islam; one of them being this very narration, famously recognised as 'the narration of intentions'.[1]

The great scholar, 'Abd ar-Rahman ibn Mahdi RA would advise authors to initiate every chapter of their book with this very narration; thus serving as a reminder to

[1] Kashf al-Mushkil

the individual and their audience to rectify their intentions even when reading and studying a book.[2]

Imam 'Abdullah ibn al-Mubarak ﵀ mentioned, 'Any small action becomes magnified due to a good intention preceding it, whereas many great actions become insignificant (and devoid of reward) due to a lacking in the presence of a correct intention that precedes the action', this is from amongst the many statements of the scholars that highlight the necessity of rectifying the intention.[3]

This applies to even the smallest of acts of goodness, if an individual was to clean away dirt from the floor with the basis of their action being the protection of the creation of Allah and to save them from harm, then this action of removing the dirt will become very valuable and appreciated by Almighty Allah. Picking up litter may seem seriously insignificant, nevertheless, the purity of intention has rendered it as extremely valuable.

On the other hand, if an individual performs one of the most noble of deeds such as the performance of a two-unit prayer, however, this action of his is void of an intention altogether or his intention is corrupt (he intends to pray so he can showcase his piety to the people), then this great and noble act of prayer will not be a means of reward for him, rather, he may even receive sin for this action as he had a corrupt intention.

A great scholar by the name of Salim RA once received a letter of advice from the leader of the Muslims, Umar ibn Abdul Aziz RA. He wrote thus; 'Know that the help of Almighty Allah is apportioned in accordance to the intentions of the individual'.[4]

He is indicating that if an individual has high aspirations and lofty intentions, then Almighty Allah will help him fulfil those intentions. On the other hand, if an individual does not have high hopes or he fails to construct correct intentions then Almighty Allah will not assist him in his actions.

Imam Ghazaali RA highlights the importance of making an intention by explaining that the mere formulation of a correct intention is a means of reward, even if he does not complete the good action. However, if he fulfils the action (which he intended to do) then upon completion of that action he will receive ten rewards.[5]

---

[2] 'Umdah al-Qari
[3] Jami' al-'Ulum wal-Hikam
[4] Az-Zuhd by Imam Ahmad, narration number 1761.
[5] Ihya 'Ulum ad-Din.

The Prophet ﷺ mentions in a narration,

Almighty Allah does not look at the external appearance of an individual, nor their wealth when deciding on the apportioning of rewards; rather He looks at the hearts (sincerity of intentions) and the deeds of an individual (and it's conformity with the Quran and Sunnah) when deciding to reward.[6]

Scholars of the past would make considerable effort in an attempt to improve and perfect their intentions just as one works on improving other physical actions and skills.

A devotee by the name of Sahl RA was once asked his thoughts in regard to the most difficult of actions for an individual, he replied, 'The rectification of the intention (and making one's action purely for Allah), as the ego has no benefit in the rectification of intentions!'[7]

The scholar Abu Sulaymaan ad-Daraani RA mentions, 'When an individual continues to rectify their intentions, then Almighty Allah will remove the disease of bad thoughts (doubts) from their heart'.[8]

Finally, it is important to note that the real place for making the intention is the heart, one should constantly ponder upon the action he is performing and remind himself, 'For whom is this action of mine?'

---

[6] Sahih Muslim

[7] Bustaan al-'Arifeen

[8] ar-Risaalah al-Qushayriyyah

أَكْمَلُ الْمُؤْمِنِيْنَ إِيْمَانًا أَحْسَنُهُمْ خُلُقًا

The most perfect of believers is the one with the best of manners ***(Sahih at-Tirmidhi)***

The rectification of one's manners is a pivotal aspect of Islam. One should display good manners to every individual; ranging from one's parents, one's husband or wife, one's children, and even towards non-Muslims. The manners of Islam are not limited to humans, rather they extend to even animals, plants, trees and every other creation of Almighty Allah. The Quran itself describes the conduct of the Prophet ﷺ,

> *Verily, you are upon the best of manners.*[9]

The Companion Abu Dharr رضي الله عنه mentions that the Prophet ﷺ mentioned,

> *Fear Allah in all places, whenever you commit a sin (or a mistake), follow it up with a good deed, the good deed will remove the harms of the bad deed, and treat people with good manners.*[10]

In this narration, the Prophet ﷺ has ordered the Muslims to treat all people with the best of manners. Just as the prophet ﷺ commanded us to perform the prayer, to give in charity, to perform the pilgrimage; he also ordered us to treat everyone with the best of manners.

In another narration the Prophet ﷺ emphasises this principle further, he does so whilst addressing the men in regard to their treatment of women. The Prophet ﷺ mentions,

> *The best believer is the one who possesses the best of manners, and the best from them is the one that is the best to his women.*[11]

It is common practice today for many to be neglectful of the rights of the women folk, some are even harsh and cruel to them. The Prophet ﷺ clearly emphasised the importance of treating them fairly and with impeccable manners. The Prophet ﷺ mentions,

> *Indeed, manners are distributed amongst the people just as the food and sustenance is distributed amongst the people.*[12]

---

[9] Surah al-Qalam, chapter 68, verse 4.
[10] Sunan at-Tirmidhi, vol 3 page 235, Hadeeth number 2102.
[11] Sunan at-Tirmidhi, vol 2 page 360, Hadeeth number 1194.

The mother of the believers, 'Aa-ishah RA was once asked regarding the character of the Prophet ﷺ, she replied, 'His character was the Quran!'[13]

She intended a very profound meaning with this statement, such that if one were to read the Quran with deep understanding and contemplation whilst maintaining an appreciation for the meaning and message of the Quran, then one will comprehend that the Prophet ﷺ was the practical manifestation and embodiment of the teachings found within the Quran.

In another narration the Prophet ﷺ mentioned,

> *An individual attains such a status by way of good conduct which a person would normally attain by means of consistent fasts and staying awake in prayer for nights on end!*[14]

The Prophet ﷺ himself outlines one of the major reasons for him being sent to this world, he says,

> *I have been sent only to (improve and) perfect exemplary character.*[15]

In another narration the Prophet ﷺ mentions,

> *The most beloved to me and the closest to me on the day of Judgment will be the person who has the best of manners.*[16]

This emphasis in regard to good character is not only emphasised by the Prophet ﷺ, but it was a consistent theme amongst his Companions and the scholars after them too, the fourth caliph, Ali ؓ would mention that good manners is the implementation of three principles:

1. Abstention from the prohibitions,
2. The seeking of only the lawful,
3. Spending upon one's family.[17]

The great scholar, 'Abdullah bin Mubarak ؓ defined good manners as the meeting of people with a cheerful face, spending on that which is a means of goodness and to avoid causing harm (to others).[18]

---

[12] Musnad Ahmad
[13] Saheeh Muslim
[14] Sunan abu Dawood
[15] Musad Ahmad
[16] Sunan at-Tirmidhi, vol 3 page 247, Hadeeth number 2137.
[17] Ihya 'Uloom ad-Deen
[18] Jami' al-'Uloom wal-Hikam

Imam Ahmad RA used to define good manners as the abstention from anger and hatred.[19]

Hafidh Ibn al-Qayyim RA mentions that the Prophet ﷺ possessed two great qualities, god-consciousness and good manners. He then explains that god-consciousness perfects the relationship between the slave and Almighty Allah, hence a person of god-consciousness is loved by Almighty Allah, whereas good manners perfects the relationship between an individual and other people, hence a person of good manners is loved by the people.[20]

[19] Jami' al-'Uloom wal-Hikam

[20] al-Adab ash-Shar'iyyah

اَلطُّهُوْرُ شَطْرُ الْاِيْمَانِ

Purification is half of faith

(Sahih Muslim)

Islam provides guidance regarding all aspects relevant to an individual's life, one of these features includes the purity of an individual, purity consists of both; the esoteric purity (i.e. internal purity such that it is only understood by the knowledgeable) along with exoteric purity (i.e. external purity such that it is easily understood by the laity).

The esoteric purity includes the correcting of one's beliefs and working on removing evil traits, the likes of jealousy, hypocrisy, hatred, etc.[21]

Almighty Allah mentions in the Quran, 'Collect charity from them; for it will purify them.'[22] Commentators of the exegesis of this verse mention that the collecting of charity will be a means of purifying them from their sins.[23]

The Companion, Abdullah ibn Umar ﷺ mentions, 'Once the ruling of charity was made, Almighty Allah made charity a cause of purifying one's wealth.'[24]

It is of imperative importance that a person makes every effort to purify their esoteric being whilst simultaneously working on the exoteric body too, it is only after the acquisition of inner purification that an individual will begin to appreciate and experience the sweetness of worship and faith.

The third Caliph, Uthman ﷺ makes mentions, 'If our hearts were purified, then we would never be negligent and deficient in the reading of the Quran (rather, we would strive to read more of the Quran as the sweetness of the Qur'an would penetrate our hearts).'[25]

Almighty Allah mentions in the Quran that he loves those that adopt a life of purity, Abul 'Aaliyah RA mentions in the exegesis of this verse, 'The quality of purity in water is desired, but Allah loves those that purify themselves from sins.'[26]

---

[21] Mirqát al-Mafátíh
[22] Qurán, Surah at-Tawbah, 103
[23] ad-Dur al-Manthúr
[24] Sahih al-Bukhari
[25] Igaathah al-Lahfaan
[26] Tafsir ibn Kathir

The purification of the exoteric qualities includes the cleanliness and purification of one's clothes and body from impurities, the performance of ablution prior to the prayer etc.

In one Prophetic narration the Prophet ﷺ has mentioned, 'Wear white clothes as it is cleaner and superior.'[27]

Commentators mention that white clothing is the more superior clothing, it was the colour the angels would wear when they used to come to this world and greet with the noble prophets, the Prophet ﷺ himself would prefer donning white clothing and would encourage others upon the wearing of white.[28]

The great scholar ibn al-Qayyim mentions, 'If an individual meets their Lord in the hereafter in a state of purity, without any dirt, then they will directly enter into Paradise. However, if an individual meets their Lord with permanent impurities (of disbelief), then they will never enter Paradise, and if a person meets their Lord with temporary impurities (of sin), then they will be cleansed first and then entered into paradise with a delay.'[29]

Scholars have mentioned many benefits of purity; these include:

1. Gaining the pleasure of Allah,
2. A higher degree of perfection in a number of acts of worship,
3. Strengthening of the body,
4. Improvement of hygiene standards within the society.

[27] Sunan at-Tirmidhi, vol 4 page 103, Hadeeth number 3014.
[28] 'Umdaul Qari
[29] Igaathah al-Lahfaan

أَفْشُوْا السَّلَامَ بَيْنَكُمْ

Spread Salaam (the Islamic greeting) amongst yourselves

(Sahih Muslim)

Spreading the Islamic greeting of peace is consistently emphasised by the Prophet ﷺ and the jurists RA.

In one narration, the Prophet ﷺ mentioned,

'You will not enter Jannah until you believe, and you will not be of (complete) belief until you love one and other'. The Prophet ﷺ then asked the Companions, 'What shall increase your love for one and other?' The Prophet ﷺ answered himself, 'Spread Salaam amongst yourselves (and it shall increase the love between one another).[30]

Qadhi 'Iyadh RA mentions, 'Salaam is the first stage towards affection and is the key for love'.[31]

The Prophet ﷺ never restricted his salaam to the elderly and the senior members of the community only, rather, the Prophet ﷺ would express his humble nature by greeting even the young with salaam. The great Companion Anas رضي الله عنه passed by some of the youth and he greeted them with salaam, he then mentioned, 'The Prophet ﷺ would greet the youth with salaam too'.[32]

The master of Hadeeth, Ibn al-Mulaqqin RA mentions, '(The objective of the Prophet's ﷺ greeting the youth was) to train one's soul and teach it humility by removing pride (and the Prophet ﷺ became a physical manifestation of this practice for his followers)'.[33]

The Prophet ﷺ informed his followers regarding the individual who is the most beloved to Almighty Allah; 'The closest in proximity to Allah is the one who initiates the salaam'.[34]

The great scholar, Zayn ad-Din al-Munaawi RA mentions, 'The reason for this proximity to Allah is because salaam is a dhikr (a form of remembrance) in and of

---

[30] Sahih Muslim
[31] Ikmaal al-Mu'lim
[32] Sahih al-Bukhari
[33] At-Tawdeeh
[34] Sunan abu-Dawud

itself, it is the greeting of peace specific to the Muslim and is also the practice of the Prophets'.[35]

The second Caliph, Umar ﵁ mentioned, 'Three actions will enable you to cultivate love for your brother;

1. Greeting them with salaam upon meeting them,
2. Creating space for them in a gathering when they join,
3. Calling them with a name that they prefer.[36]

The vizier, Ibn Hubairah RA mentioned, 'Whoever greets an individual with salaam, then he is protected from all his harms.'[37]

Mentioning an etiquette of salaam, the fourth Caliph, 'Ali ﵁ mentioned, 'If a group passes by, then it will suffice an individual from amongst them to give the salaam and for one amongst those sitting to reply'.[38]

---

[35] Faydh al-Qadeer
[36] A'dab al-'Ushrah
[37] al-Adab ash-Shar'iyyah
[38] Sunan abu-Dawud

لَا تَغْضَبْ

Do not become angry

(Sahih Bukhari)

The Prophet ﷺ has mentioned,

> *'Indeed, anger is from the (acts of the) Devil and the Devil is a creation of Hell-Fire, the fire of Hell will be extinguished with water, hence, when one of you becomes angry then perform the ritual ablution (i.e. the water will extinguish the anger)'.*[39]

The Prophet ﷺ has also mentioned,

> *'When one of you gets angry whilst they are standing, then they should sit, if this does not aid in the removal of the anger, then they should lie down'.*[40]

Upon occasion, two individuals were arguing in the presence of the Prophet ﷺ, one of them was furious with the other and the anger was visible on his face. At this juncture, the Prophet ﷺ informed the Companions, 'I am aware of a statement, if the person with anger were to recite it, his anger would be removed; that statement is, "I seek refuge with the help of Allah from the Devil".[41]

The Prophet ﷺ himself would seek refuge from the anger of Almighty Allah, it is reported in a narration that when thunder or lightning would strike, the Prophet ﷺ would supplicate, 'Oh Allah, do not destroy us with Your anger or punishment, forgive us (and grant us peace)'.[42]

The Prophet ﷺ would advise his people to 'educate the masses, create ease for them, remain silent when a person becomes angry with you'.[43]

The Prophet ﷺ mentioned, 'When Allah created the creation, He wrote in a paper that was kept by Him, "Indeed, my mercy has surpassed my anger"'.

---

[39] Sunan abu-Dawud
[40] Sunan abu-Dawud
[41] Sahih al-Bukhari
[42] Sunan at-Tirmidhi, vol 4 page 462, Hadeeth number 3738.
[43] Musnad Ahmed

The Prophet ﷺ further educated us thus, 'Power (and might) is not in the defeating of others, rather it is in the controlling of one's anger at the time of rage'.[44]

The just, great ruler, 'Umar ibn 'Abdul 'Aziz RA would command his governors and judges, 'Do not mete out a punishment in the state of anger, only punish once the anger has subsided'.[45]

The Imam, Ja'far as-Sadiq RA is quoted to have said, 'Anger is the key to all evil'.[46]

Hafidh ibn al-Qayyim RA mentioned,

> *'People will enter the doors of Hell-fire from three entrances; the door of doubt; which will be the entrance of those that doubted the religion of Allah, the door of desires; which will be the entrance of those that followed their desires above the divine law, and the door of anger; wherein those who used to oppress the creation of Allah as a result of their anger will enter from'.*[47]

The wise have advised, 'The anger which an individual cannot control is (a sign of) weakness, and the anger which an individual can control is a (sign of) disgrace (for him as the anger will make him commit actions that will humiliate him).'[48] Therefore, doing actions and deeds in the state of anger, will more often than not, bring about humiliation and regret.

A scholar once mentioned, 'Beware of anger, for indeed, it eventually forces an individual to the formulation of excuses (as he will soon regret the actions he committed in the state of anger)!'[49]

---

[44] Sahih al-Bukhari
[45] Ihya 'Ulum ad-Din
[46] Ihya 'Ulum ad-Din
[47] Al-Fawaaid
[48] Aadaab ad-Dunya wad Din
[49] Ihya 'Ulum ad-Din

إِنَّ اللهَ رَفِيْقٌ يُحِبُّ الرِّفْقَ

Allah is gentle and loves the quality of gentleness

(Sahih Muslim)

This Prophetic narration emphasises the importance of showing compassion towards the creation of Almighty Allah.

Imam Muslim RA reports a narration in which the Prophet ﷺ mentioned,

> *'Be cautious of oppression, for indeed oppression will be a means of darkness in the hereafter'.*[50]

The Prophet ﷺ has even advised kindness in regard to the treatment of one's servants or workers,

> *'When your servant brings you food, then make him sit and partake in it with you, and if you do not make him sit and eat with you, then at least give him a morsel or two to eat; after all, he has gone through the hardship of preparing this food'.*[51]

The women in pre-Islamic Arabia were treated extremely harshly and inhumanely and so the Prophet ﷺ would emphasise, 'Hold firm onto my advice regarding the treatment of the women folk with goodness'.[52]

When the Prophet ﷺ sent Mu'aadh ibn Jabal رضي الله عنه on an expedition to preach Islam, the Prophet ﷺ advised a number of things;

> *'Call the people towards Islam, educate them regarding prayer and charity, thereafter, ensure that during your term in office you remain cautious of the curse of any person who is oppressed because there is no veil between the call of the oppressed and Almighty Allah (their call is accepted immediately)'.*[53]

The Prophet ﷺ also gave similar advices to members of the public;

> *'Refrain from having suspicions regarding others, do not spy on others, do not compete (in a manner which leads to hatred and enmity), stay away from*

[50] Sahih Muslim
[51] Sahih al-Bukhari
[52] Sahih al-Bukhari
[53] Sahih al-Bukhari

jealousy, do not harbour hatred for one another, rather, live with one another as brothers'.[54]

'Aishah RA mentions a story of a woman that came to her with two young girls in search of food, 'Aishah RA had nothing except for three dates which she offered, the woman took the three dates and gave a date each to her two daughters and intended to consume the third herself. As she was about to consume her date, the daughters began to ask her for it, she divided the date in two and gave it to her daughters. When the Prophet ﷺ returned home, 'Aishah RA mentioned the incident to him, upon hearing the incident the Prophet ﷺ mentioned, "Indeed that deed was so noble that Almighty Allah has made paradise compulsory upon her'.[55]

This theme has remained consistent in the previous religions too, a person from the earlier religions was accounted for his deeds by Almighty Allah, the person had nothing good to show in his deeds except that he was rich and used to order his workers to forgive the poor of any financial burden; upon this single act Almighty Allah mentioned, 'I am more worthy of this act (of forgiving), so forgive him (and enter him into paradise)'.

A person advised the great caliph, 'Umar ibn Abdul Azeez RA, 'Deal with the senior members of the community as though they are your own father, the younger members as your sons, and those of a similar age to you as your brothers; which one from your father, son or brother would you deal with in a bad (and harsh) manner?'[56]

---

[54] Sahih al-Bukhari
[55] Sahih al-Muslim
[56] Jami' al-'Uloom wal-Hikam

السَّعِيْدُ مَنْ وُعِظَ بِغَيْرِهِ

The fortunate one is the one who takes advice from others

(Sahih Muslim)

Allah has placed lessons and signs in everything around us, whether we look into our own lives or the lives of those around us, there are numerous lessons one can learn, to the extent that we can even take heed if we ponder upon the lives of those that have passed before us.

Almighty Allah mentions, 'Indeed, those people that transgressed in regard to the Sabbath (Saturday), we said to them, 'Become disgraced monkeys, and we made them a deterrent for those who were present and those who succeeded them, and (we made them) a lesson for the God-fearing (that one must always follow the commands set by Almighty Allah).

The Prophet ﷺ advised his followers in regard to every aspect of their lives, whether from an individual perspective or a societal perspective, therefore, it is in the benefit of any individual to take the advice of the Prophet ﷺ above all other advices.

Once, a person came to the Prophet ﷺ revealing that he deliberately misses the Fajr prayer due to the Imam (as he was extending his recitation beyond the prescribed Sunnah amount), the Prophet ﷺ became extremely upset and concerned, he then instructed the companions,

> *'Oh people! Verily from amongst you there are those that are distancing people from the religion. He who leads the prayer should make it short (and in conformity to the Sunnah prescribed amount), (remember that) the elderly, weak and labourers (who have worked the entire day) pray behind you'.*[57]

On another occasion, the Prophet ﷺ advised, 'Oh people, be kind and merciful to the womenfolk (something that was unheard of in the pre-Islamic era)'.[58]

Once, 'Umar bin 'Abdul 'Azeez RA began weeping whilst sat in a gathering, the people enquired as to the reason for his weeping and he explained thus,

> *'I pondered deeply upon the world, its bounties and the desires within it, the deeper I pondered, the greater the lessons I learnt in regard to refraining from it (and its desires). The desires of this world come to end after becoming old*

[57] Sahih al-Bukhari

[58] Sunan at-Tirmidhi, vol 2 page 361, Hadeeth number 1195.

and unfashionable. For indeed, in the world and its inclinations are lessons and advices for those who understand'.[59]

Abu Muhriz at-Tanaawi has made mention, 'The (visiting of the) graveyard should suffice you as an advice in regards to those who have passed'.[60]

[59] Tafsir ibn Kathir
[60] Adab ad-Dunya wad Deen

الدُّعَاءُ هُوَ الْعِبَادَةُ

Dua' (supplication) is worship

(Sunan Abu Dawood)

Supplication and making a prayer is an integral aspect of our religion, when an individual supplicates, they submit before Almighty Allah and display their absolute helplessness and neediness towards Him. Almighty Allah is the possessor of absolute power and might and therefore He is the being that all mankind are dependant of.

Almighty Allah mentions, 'Supplicate to Me (call upon Me), I will answer your call'.

The Prophet ﷺ has educated the significance of supplication and its prominence in the religion by reminding us, 'Nothing is more valuable to Almighty Allah than the supplication (of a believer)'.[61]

The Prophet ﷺ has advised in regard to a number of etiquettes that are relative to supplication in various narrations. He mentions,

> *'Whoever wishes that their supplication be accepted at a time of difficulty and hardship, then they should supplicate during the times of happiness (a person should show their neediness to Almighty Allah at moments of happiness, Almighty Allah will remember them at their time of difficulty)'.*[62]

After an individual has supplicated, they should not complain if their prayer has not been accepted in the form they expected and hoped for, Almighty Allah can accept a supplication in different ways, it is possible the acceptance of that supplication has been delayed by Almighty Allah for the benefit of the servant. The Prophet ﷺ mentioned, 'The supplications of the people are accepted for as long as they do not complain regarding a supplication not being accepted immediately'.[63]

There are certain moments when the supplications of an individual have a greater chance of acceptance, one of these moments is the supplication made in the final portion of the night, Almighty Allah descends to the skies and asks, 'Who will call upon Me, so that I may respond to their call? Who will ask from Me so that I may provide for them? Who will seek forgiveness from Me so that I may forgive them?'[64]

---

[61] Sunan at-Tirmidhi, vol 4 page 423, Hadeeth number 3653.

[62] At-Tabrani

[63] Sahih al-Bukhari

[64] Sahih al-Bukhari

It is important that the supplicating person sends peace and salutations upon the Prophet ﷺ at the initiation and completion of their prayer. Abu Sulayman ad-Daaraani RA has made mention,

> *'Whosoever intends to ask from Almighty Allah their needs, then they should send peace and salutations upon the Prophet ﷺ at the beginning of their prayer, only then should they ask their needs, thereafter one should conclude their supplication with peace and salutations upon the Prophet ﷺ; for without a doubt, Almighty Allah will accept the peace and salutations made upon his Prophet ﷺ, and the Lord is Merciful, so why would he reject the prayer made in between the two accepted salutations'.*[65]

[65] Ihya 'Uloom ad-Din

مَنْ صَمَتَ نَجَا

The individual who remains silent, has saved himself

(Sunan at-Tirmidhi)

Prophet Muhammad ﷺ has mentioned, 'Whoever believes in Allah and the last day should speak good (that which is beneficial to both oneself and others) or remain silent, whoever has believed in Allah and the last day should treat their neighbours with care, whoever has believed in Allah and the last day should honour their guests'.[66]

The Companion, Al-Harith ibn Hisham ؓ asked the Prophet ﷺ for some advice to assist himself to refrain from sins, the Prophet ﷺ pointed to the tongue and said, 'Control this'.[67]

The famous Companion, Ibn 'Abbas ؓ admonished himself saying, 'Oh tongue! Speak good (that which is beneficial) and you shall benefit, otherwise, remain silent from any evil talk, for only then shall you be saved from regretting anything'.[68]

The Prophet ﷺ was once asked, 'Which Muslim is the best?' The Prophet ﷺ replied, 'The one whose tongue or hands do not harm others'.[69]

The Prophet ﷺ informed us regarding three actions that Almighty Allah dislikes; gossip, excessive questioning (which is not productive nor beneficial) and the wasting of money.[70]

Prophet Sulaiman عليه السلام mentioned, 'If your speech reaches the value of silver (meaning the speech is good and beneficial, but not gold), then know that your silence is gold (i.e. in most cases silence is the better option)'.[71]

The second caliph, Umar ibn al-Khattab ؓ used to mention, 'When an individual's speech increases, there is a tendency that their mistakes will also increase'.[72]

The great Companion, 'Abdullah ibn Mas'ood ؓ would mention, 'By Allah, nothing is more in need of a lengthy imprisonment than the tongue'.[73]

---

[66] Sahih al-Bukhari
[67] Al-Mu'jam al-Kabeer
[68] Shu'ab al-Imaan
[69] Sahih al-Bukhari
[70] Sahih al-Bukhari
[71] Ihya 'Ulum ad-Din
[72] As-Samt

The jurist, Taawoos RA was known for his quiet nature, when asked regarding this habit of his, he would mention, 'I have tested (and experienced) the way of the tongue for many years and have always found it to be mischievous'.[74]

Once, the pious saint, Muhammad ibn Wasi' RA advised his student, Malik ibn Dinar RA, 'The safeguarding of the tongue is harder for the people than the safeguarding of their money'.[75]

It is evident from these practices of the pious scholars and Companions that they gave great importance to the safeguarding of the tongue, as it is the tongue that leads individuals to many sins. Lying, backbiting, swearing, verbally disgracing, scolding, scorning, mocking, slandering, these are just few of the sins **directly** committed by the tongue, there are even more sins which are caused by the bad words that are uttered by the mouth and then leads to disagreements, hatred or even fights.

---

[73] Ihya 'Ulum ad-Din

[74] As-Samt

[75] Ihya 'Ulum ad-Din

لَا يَدْخُلُ الْجَنَّةَ قَاطِعٌ

The one who breaks relationships will not enter paradise

(Sahih al-Bukhari)

One of the fundamental teachings of Islam is to establish amicable and friendly ties with family members, neighbours and all people in society, Islam has strongly emphasised upon the building of a noble and righteous society.

The importance of establishing ties, especially with relatives is emphasised by the Prophet ﷺ with such vigour that it is second only to belief (imaan). Once, a man came to the Prophet ﷺ and asked him, 'Which action is the most beloved to Almighty Allah?' The Prophet ﷺ responded, 'Belief (imaan) in Allah'. The man then asked for the second most beloved action, the Prophet ﷺ informed him, 'Establishing ties with relatives'. When the person asked for the third most beloved action, the Prophet ﷺ responded, 'Enjoin others towards good deeds and forbid them from evil'.[76]

The Prophet ﷺ mentioned that the deeds of all humans are presented before Almighty Allah every Thursday night, the (good) deeds of those that sever the ties of kinship are not accepted.[77]

It is important to understand that the perfecting of ties with relatives is not a matter of merely maintaining good relations with those that are amicable towards you, rather, it is when a person persists in doing good with the one who severs ties with you, that is the reality of the definition 'maintaining good ties' and is rewarded greatly by Almighty Allah.[78]

Whilst living amongst different people who have a multitude of backgrounds, mind-sets and thoughts, then it is very possible that differences of opinions will occur and disagreements will take place, however, there is immense reward for the maintaining of ties especially in difficult times, and there is even more reward for maintaining ties when they themselves sever ties and relations with you.

---

[76] At-Targheeb wat-Tarheeb
[77] Musnad Ahmad
[78] Sahih al-Bukhari

The caliph, 'Umar ibn 'Abdul 'Azeez RA strongly advised the scholar Maymoon ibn Mahraan to avoid breaking ties with his relatives, for indeed Almighty Allah has cursed the people who break ties twice in the Holy Qur'an.[79]

The scholar, at-Teebi RA mentioned, 'The effects of maintaining ties (and strengthening relations) are long-lasting, Allah does not allow the positive effects of such a great deed to vanish so quickly'.[80]

The Prophet ﷺ mentioned, 'The individual who desires that provisions (wealth etc.) is increased for him and his life be prolonged, then that individual should maintain good relations with kinship'.[81]

'Allamah al-'Ayni RA has mentioned three possible explanations for the increasing in an individual's life due to the keeping of good ties:

The first is that the blessings in their life will increase, thus allowing them to increase in their opportunities to do good deeds, so, despite the fact that the actual number of years spent on this earth will not increase, the additional blessings in their life will make their life much more valuable and productive.

The second is that the lifespan itself increases, and so after Almighty Allah has decreed a specific age for an individual, Allah then informs the angels in regard to the individual's lifespan, however, if the person maintains good ties with his relatives then the age will increase by a certain number of years, if the person maintains ties with even more relatives, then this age will increase by a greater number of years, and so on. So the age, in reality, will increase by the maintenance of good ties, although the knowledge of Almighty Allah is such that He is already aware of the exact number of relationships every individual will maintain, hence, He already has the knowledge of how many years the individual will eventually live even though the angels may not have been informed regarding this exact number.

The third is that the individual will die at their normal age, however, even after dying, due to the maintenance of good ties with the people, the people will continue praising the individual even after their death, in essence, their name will continue to live on and they will be respected amongst society.[82]

---

[79] Masawi' al-Akhlaaq

[80] Al-Kashif 'an Haqaaiq as-Sunan

[81] Saheeh al-Bukhari, narration number 5986.

[82] 'Umdah al-Qari'

نِعْمَتَانِ مَغْبُوْنٌ فِيْهِمَا كَثِيْرٌ مِنَ النَّاسِ الصِّحَّةُ وَالْفَرَاغِ

Many are deceived regarding two favours; good health and free time

(Sahih al-Bukhari)

Almighty Allah has bestowed us with innumerable bounties and favours, the Qur'an testifies to this; 'And if you count the favour(s) of Almighty Allah (upon you), you would not (be able to) enumerate them, indeed Allah is Forgiving and Merciful'.[83]

Hafidh ibn Katheer RA indicates that Almighty Allah has bestowed us with so many favours that if an individual were ordered to thank Him for all the favours bestowed upon us, then they would be incapable of thanking Him, it is for this reason that Almighty Allah actually forgives the numerous bounties we show ingratitude for and rewards us for the few bounties we do show gratitude for.[84]

The Prophet ﷺ has informed us that amongst the numerous favours from Almighty Allah upon us, two favours worth mentioning are 'good health' and 'free time', if an individual fails to derive the maximum benefit from these two favours during his existence in this world, then he is at a great loss.

'Allamah ibn Battal RA advises that the method of deriving the utmost benefit from and avoiding major losses in this world is in recognising that Almighty Allah created the human race (and all other creations) without the slightest need or dependence to them, thereafter, He bestowed the human race with numerous favours above all other creations; without the human race being deserving of such favours. He further bestowed human beings with health and intellect, he provided sustenance for them and for every good act they performed, He magnified their rewards and for any evil they committed, the punishment was not multiplied.

Almighty Allah then ordered the people to worship Him and to ponder upon His innumerable favours, He instructed them to show gratitude with simple formulae and a few acts of daily worship. Despite the many favours, He only expected from the human being that they worship Him for a limited period within this temporal life, and in return He promised an infinite reward in the hereafter. If an individual was to truly appreciate these bounties and to take advantage of them, then he would use every spare moment in this life and every iota of strength in the obedience of Allah in order to acquire the vast and infinite reward of the hereafter.[85]

It is imperative to keep in mind the temporal nature of this world, or else one may easily lose focus and begin chasing this world, rather, aim to be content with whatever little or large Almighty Allah has given us and then use as much of this 'free time' and 'good health' in the obedience of Allah. The Prophet ﷺ mentioned, 'Whoever wakes up with the feeling of security (within himself and his

---

[83] Surah an-Nahl, ayah 18.
[84] Tafseer ibn Katheer, vol 4, page 562.
[85] Sharh Ibn Battal, vol 10, page 147.

family), has good health and has food for the day, then indeed he has acquired all of this (important and necessary aspects of this) world'.[86]

In another narration, the Prophet ﷺ informed us that the first bounty and favour of Almighty Allah that we will be asked regarding on the day of reckoning will be the good health that Allah has blessed us with.[87]

When the great Companion, Ibn 'Abbas ﷺ was asked regarding the verse, 'Then on that day (of reckoning) you will be asked regarding the bounties (Almighty Allah bestowed you with),'[88] Ibn Abbas ﷺ explained that it refers to the healthy body, ears, eyes, etc. that Almighty Allah had given to the human, they will then be asked regarding how they spent these bounties.[89]

We should strive and use every bounty Almighty Allah has given to us in a manner that proves productive and beneficial to ourselves and even those around us, that includes seeing the lawful and keeping our gazes away from the unlawful, listening to the lawful (i.e. Qur'an, good lessons, good talks, etc.) and keeping our ears away from listening to the unlawful (i.e. backbiting, gossip, etc.).

It is imperative that we make every effort we can in recognising as many favours of Almighty Allah upon us, this will pave the way for a greater zeal and fervour in our worship, but it will also become a form of encouragement for us to increase in the quality of our devotion to Him and it will enhance our appreciation and love for Him further. A person came to the scholar, Yunus ibn 'Abeed RA and they complained regarding the difficult times and financial hardship he was suffering. Yunus ibn 'Abeed RA simply asked him, 'Would you be pleased if I were to take your eyesight away from you and give you a hundred thousand (of a currency) in exchange', the individual immediately replied in the negative. Then Yunus ibn 'Abeed RA asked a similar question in regards to the ear, the heart, the hands and the feet, the person replied in the negative for all of the questions. Thereafter, Yunus ibn 'Abeed RA reminded him that these questions prove that your body is much more valuable than thousands upon thousands (of the unit of currency) yet you only find the time to complain![90]

---

[86] Sunan at-Tirmidhi, vol 3 page 421, Hadeeth number 2502.
[87] Sunan at-Tirmidhi, vol 4 page 415, Hadeeth number 3640.
[88] Surah at-Takathur, ayah number 8.
[89] Tafseer at-Tabari, narration number 38230.
[90] Sifah as-Safwah, vol 3, page 305.

رِضَى الرَّبِّ فِيْ رِضَى الْوَالِدِ وَسَخَطُ الرَّبِّ فِيْ سَخَطِ الْوَالِدِ

The happiness of Allah lies in the happiness of the parents and the displeasure of Allah lies in the displeasure of the parents

(Sahih at-Tirmidhi)

Obedience to one's parents and treating them in a kind and loving manner has been strongly emphasised by Almighty Allah, it has been mentioned a number of times in the Qur'an immediately after the order of religious monotheism (believing in the oneness of Almighty Allah).

Almighty Allah mentions, 'Worship Allah and associate nothing with Allah, and do good (be loving) with parents'.[91]

The scholar, Ibn 'Aashoor RA comments that one can derive the importance of being kind to parents even from the mere chronology of this verse, it is second only to the direct worship of Almighty Allah Himself.[92]

In the narration of Sahih al-Bukhari, the Prophet ﷺ mentions that obedience to the parents is the second most beloved deed to Almighty Allah, only second to performing the compulsory prayers at their correct times.[93]

The scholar, as-Sam'aani RA mentions, 'Obedience to the parents means being soft and gentle with them, not raising your voice above their voice, and to not answer them in the negative (when they ask something from you); in conclusion, one should be like an obedient slave before them!'[94]

The Prophet ﷺ also informed the Companion 'Umar ibn Khattab رضي الله عنه, 'The best of the Tabi'een (those individuals who met the Companions of the Prophet ﷺ) is Uwais, he had his mother living with him... ask him to seek forgiveness on behalf of you (from Almighty Allah)'.[95] Uwais al-Qarani was a saint from Yemen who was living in the era of the Prophet ﷺ and had accepted Islam, he had nothing in Yemen which was stopping him from migrating to spend time in the blessed company of the Prophet ﷺ except for his weak mother who he was busy in the service of, and so he never made the migration and was unable to meet the Prophet ﷺ due to these

---

[91] Surah an-Nisa', ayah 36.
[92] At-Tahreer wat-Tanweer, vol 4, page 123.
[93] Saheeh al-Bukhari, vol 1, page 140.
[94] Tafseer as-Sama'ni, vol 1 page 425.
[95] Saheeh Muslim, narration number 6655.

responsibilities. However, the Prophet ﷺ advised his Companions of a time when they would eventually arrive to these lands and they would meet him, that they should then ask him to supplicate for them to Allah – as he is a great saint who only missed out on the status of being a Companion of the Prophet ﷺ due to his relentless service towards his mother![96]

A person came and asked the famous Companion Ibn 'Abbas ؓ how he should repent for a major sin that he had committed, Ibn 'Abbas ؓ enquired from him if his mother was still alive, thereafter, Ibn 'Abbas ؓ explained by saying, 'I am unaware of any action more noble to Almighty Allah than the service rendered towards the mother (to the extent that it removes even the major sins from an individual)'.[97]

Imam Ahmad RA makes mention, 'Obedience to the parents removes the major sins of an individual'.[98]

The historian, Wahb ibn Munabbah RA also adds, 'The service towards parents and being gentle with them increases the life-span of an individual'.[99]

The obedience to the parents is imperative and takes priority so long as it does not result in the violation of any of the commands of Almighty Allah. For example, if the parents command the child to renounce belief in the oneness of Allah, then in this case the parents will not be obeyed as their order is in direct contradiction to the commands of Almighty Allah.

Hasan Basri RA was asked regarding the definition of 'obedience of the parents' upon which he replied, 'Spend upon your parents whatever you have (to the extent which they are in need of) and be obedient to them in all their commands except those which lead to sin'.[100]

---

[96] Tareekh al-Islam by ad-Dhahabi, vol 3, page 557 and Siyar 'A'laa an-Nubala' by ad-Dhahabi, vol 7, page 16.

[97] Al-Adab al-Mufrad, narration number 4.

[98] Ghidha al-albaab, vol 1, page 299.

[99] Ad-Durr al-Manthoor, vol 9, page 314.

[100] Musannaf 'Abd ar-Razzaq, narration number 9288.

اِتَّقُوْا اللهَ فِيْ هَذِهِ الْبَهَائِمِ الْمُعْجَمَةِ

Fear Allah in regard to these animals that cannot speak

(Sahih abu Dawood)

From amongst the innumerable favours and bounties of Almighty Allah upon us is that he has made animals such as the camel, horse, donkey etc. subservient to mankind.

Almighty Allah mentions in regard to these such animals, 'The Exalted and All-Knowing created them [...] He who has appointed for you (and made subservient to you) ships and cattle upon which you travel, in order that you may mount firmly on their backs, and that you may remember the favour of your Lord when you mount them'.[101]

The Prophet ﷺ once crossed paths with a camel that had become extremely thin and impoverished due to a lack of care, he immediately warned the individual (and mankind in general) against such cruelty to animals and explained, 'Fear (the displeasure of) Almighty Allah in regard to these animals that cannot speak (hence, they are incapable of vocalising their pains), ride them appropriately (after they have been fed and are well rested) and eat from them (after slaughtering them) appropriately (do not eat excessively and neither slaughter them in an aggressive manner, rather it should be in compliance with the standards set by the Prophet of Mercy ﷺ)'.[102]

In another narration reported by Imam Ahmad RA, the Prophet ﷺ instructed, 'Travel on the animals appropriately, allow the animals (to rest) appropriately and do not make the animals your armchairs (upon which you sit and comfortably converse with others, rather, if you have stopped to talk, then dismount and allow the animals to rest)'.[103]

The Prophet ﷺ also taught us the correct method of slaughtering the animal so that minimal pain is caused to the animal (without compromising on purity). He ﷺ mentioned, 'Almighty Allah has written upon humans that they achieve excellence in whatever they strive towards; when they slaughter the animal, it should be performed with goodness (a manner that gives least harm to the animal), (before

[101] Surah Az-Zukhruf, ayah 9-
[102] Sunan Abu Dawood, narration number 2548.
[103] Musnad Ahmad, narration number 15639.

the sacrifice) one should sharpen the knife (so that the animal does not experience prolonged pain, rather the animal dies as quickly as possible, hence, the pain is reduced) and let the animal die comfortably.'[104]

The scholar of hadeeth, Abu 'Abbas al-Qurtubi RA listed a number of etiquettes in regards to the slaughtering of the animal, 'Be gentle with the animal (as much as possible), do not force the animal to the floor in a harsh manner, do not drag the animal from one place to another, sharpen the blade (so the slaughtering can be done as quickly as possible), have the correct intention (not for merely killing an animal, rather for eating and gaining lawful energy from it so one can perform acts of goodness with that energy), face the animal towards the *Qiblah* (the direction of the sacred house in Makkah), recite the name of Almighty Allah before slaughtering it, prepare the animal for this stage (of slaughtering – don't slaughter an animal that is not prepared), [...]."[105]

The scholar, Rabee'ah RA advised, 'No animal should see a second animal being slaughtered (as it may become distressed)'.[106]

The Prophet ﷺ related a story to his Companions of a woman and he mentioned, 'She was punished (by Allah) because of a cat which she had confined and caged until it died, as a result she was made to go to hell (for the inappropriate treatment of this cat). Neither did she provide the cat with food, nor did she release the cat, allowing the cat to eat from the vermin (provisions) of the earth'.[107]

On the other hand, if an individual treats the animals in a loving and caring manner, then there is great reward for such treatment of the creation of Almighty Allah. The Prophet ﷺ mentioned that there was once a dog that was on the verge of death due to extreme thirst and it was circling a well, suddenly a sinful woman walked that way and saw the dog in this terrible state, she drew water from the well using her shoe and she gave the dog water to drink, she was forgiven due to this act of hers (and was granted paradise as a result of this).[108]

---

[104] Saheeh Muslim, narration number 5167.
[105] Al-Mufhim, vol 16, page number 140.
[106] Al-Mufhim, vol 16, page number 140.
[107] Saheeh Muslim, narration number 6841.
[108] Saheeh Muslim, narration number 5998.

الْحَيَاءُ شُعْبَةٌ مِنَ الْإِيْمَانِ

Modesty is a branch of faith

(Sahih al-Bukhari)

Modesty from a religious perspective refers to the intrinsic and innate nature of an individual which prevents them from violating any of the commands of Almighty Allah out of love and awe of their Creator.[109]

The Prophet ﷺ mentioned, 'Every religion has its distinguishing characteristics, and the distinguishing characteristic of Islam is modesty'.[110]

Almighty Allah highlights this quality of modesty and bashfulness in the Prophet ﷺ, an incident occurred when a number of Companions came and sat at the house of the Prophet ﷺ, however, they did not leave even after the fulfilment of their need, the Prophet ﷺ due to his shy nature could not tell them to disperse, however, it was troubling for the Prophet ﷺ as he had his personal duties and commitments to tend to.[111] Almighty Allah then revealed the verse, 'Oh you who have believed, do not enter the houses of the Prophet ﷺ unless you are invited for a meal, without waiting for its preparation (i.e. do not come so early that the food still needs to be prepared, rather come close to the time when it has been prepared). When you are invited, then enter (the house); and when you have eaten, disperse without seeking to remain for (lengthy and inconvenient) conversation. Indeed, that (behaviour of staying for a lengthy period of time after food) was troubling to the Prophet ﷺ, however, he is shy of (dismissing) you, but Almighty Allah is not shy from mentioning the truth'.[112]

Refraining from any violation in regard to the commands of Almighty Allah is the essence of modesty, however, following the Sunnah is also a form of modesty. A companion once came to the Prophet ﷺ and asked for some advice, the Prophet ﷺ said, 'I advise you to be modest (and practice the commands of Almighty Allah) in a similar manner to how you adopt modesty before a pious person'.[113]

When an individual lacks modesty and does not feel any shame or regret over their shortcomings then it will eventually lead them to feeling a level of independence

---

[109] At-Ta'reefat, vol 1, page 126.
[110] Sunan Ibn Majah, hadeeth number 4181.
[111] Tafseer Ibn Abi Hatim, vol 10, page 3149. Tafseer ar-Razi, vol 25, page 179.
[112] Surah al-'Ahzab, ayah 53.
[113] Az-Zuhd by Imam Ahmad, vol 1, page 46.

from Almighty Allah and they will rarely fear any reckoning. The Prophet ﷺ mentioned, 'One of the teachings learnt from the earlier prophets is that if an individual does not feel ashamed (over their sins etc.) then they will do whatever they desire (without fearing any consequences)'.[114]

This is explained by the scholar Ka'b al-Ahbar RA, he says, 'If bashfulness (and modesty) is not found in any individual, then they will be in hell fire forever (as they would have committed numerous sins and not felt the need to seek forgiveness)'.[115]

Unfortunately, when a person adopts the great quality of modesty and piety, it is common for a few who are acquainted with this individual to question his modesty and to claim that he is exceeding boundaries, however, the incident of the Prophet Musa عليه السلام should serve as a reminder for us on such occasions. The Prophet Musa عليه السلام was living in an era where nudity and semi-nudity was regarded the norm. Despite this, the Prophet Musa عليه السلام would habitually cover his entire body because of his modesty. A person attempted to insult him by saying, 'He covers his entire body because he has some defect on his skin, either he suffers from vitiligo, a scrotal hernia or some other defect!' Thereafter, Almighty Allah cleared Prophet Musa عليه السلام from this accusation (and the people came to know that they were mere slanders).[116]

Regardless of the insults and taunts of others, one should remain patient and persevere in the promotion of good, Allah will reward you and elevate you. This is echoed in another narration of the Prophet ﷺ wherein he mentions 'Modesty in its entirety is goodness'.[117]

The second Caliph, 'Umar ﷺ mentioned, 'If one's modesty (and bashfulness) decreases, then their piety will also decrease and if piety decreases then the heart will die (spiritually)'.[118]

When one adopts modesty at all times and refrains from breaking the commands of Almighty Allah, then Allah will forgive his shortcomings and failings. The great saint, Yahya ibn Mu'aadh RA mentions, 'If an individual is ashamed of (violating the commands of) Allah whilst being obedient (and remains modest at all times), then

[114] Saheeh al-Bukhari, hadeeth number 6120.
[115] Makarim al-Akhlaaq by Ibn Abi ad-Dunya, vol 1 page 43.
[116] Saheeh al-Bukhari, hadeeth number 3404.
[117] Saheeh Muslim, hadeeth number 166.
[118] Makarim al-Akhlaaq by Ibn Abi ad-Dunya, vol 1 page 40.

Almighty Allah will feel a sense of shame in regard to (disgracing) him when the individual sins'.[119]

A number of scholars have been quoted to have said, 'Raw faith is naked, its clothing is the fear of disobeying Allah (by fulfilling his commands), its decoration is adopting modesty and its fruits are knowledge'.[120]

---

[119] Madarij as-Salikeen, vol 2, page 260. This saying of Yahya ibn Muadh has been explained with different explanations.

[120] Miftah Dar as-Sa'dah, vol 1, page 122.

الْمَرْءُ مَعَ مَنْ أَحَبَّ

A person will be with whom he loves

(Sahih al-Bukhari)

A Companion once came and asked the Prophet ﷺ, 'What would you say regarding a person who loves a certain people (of the past or even the present), however, he has not met them?' The Prophet ﷺ replied, 'A person will be with whom he loves'.[121]

A Bedouin once came to the Prophet ﷺ and asked regarding the Last Hour (the day of Judgement) and how it would occur, the Prophet ﷺ wanted to advise him to stop focusing on the timing of the Last Hour, but to rather focus on what preparation he had made for the Last Hour (in terms of good deeds), and so the Prophet ﷺ asked him, 'What have you prepared for the Last Hour?' The Bedouin replied that he has not prepared many acts of worship for the Last Hour in terms of prayer, fasting, charity etc. however, he added, 'I do love Almighty Allah and his Messenger'. The Prophet ﷺ replied, 'Indeed, you will be with those (in the hereafter) whom you love'.[122]

Loving others for the sake of Almighty Allah is regarded as a sign of perfection in faith, the Prophet ﷺ mentioned, 'Loving a person for the sake of Almighty Allah and not for any financial gain, is from the (perfection of an individual's) faith'.[123]

When you truly love someone for the sake of Almighty Allah, then it is also permissible, rather, encouraged to inform them of your love (and genuine care) for them.[124] Mu'aadh ibn Jabal رضي الله عنه mentioned that once the Prophet ﷺ held his hand and said, 'Oh Mu'aadh, by Allah I love you, by Allah I love you'.[125]

There are many other methods of expressing love as well, one of those such methods is to show gratitude and to value anything the beloved has gifted you, for example, if the beloved has gifted you a watch and you wear that very same watch with the intention of expressing your gratitude and love for the person who gifted it, it is hoped that there is reward in the wearing of the watch. The fourth Caliph, 'Ali ibn abi Talib رضي الله عنه used to wear a specific set of clothes very often, he was once asked

[121] Saheeh al-Bukhari, narration number 6169.
[122] Saheeh al-Bukhari, narration number 6167.
[123] Al-Mu'jam al-Awsat by Imam Tabrani, narration number 7214.
[124] 'Awn al-Ma'bood, vol 4 page 384.
[125] Sunan Abu Dawood, narration number 1524.

regarding these clothes and so 'Ali ﷺ answered, 'My beloved friend, 'Umar ﷺ gave me these very clothes!'[126]

From amongst loving others is to love for them what you love for yourself.[127] The scholars of the past used to love for others what they regarded as the success of both worlds. Ibn 'Awn RA gives a very comprehensive set of advices, 'I love three things for myself and my brothers; (Firstly,) I love to learn the *Sunnah* (the Prophetic life) and love for others to also learn the *Sunnah* too, (secondly,) I love to learn the Qur'an and love for others to learn the Qur'an too, (thirdly,) I love to leave people alone (and not involve myself with them) except in good matters and I would also love for others the very same'.[128]

Shaykh al-Islam ibn Taymiyyah RA mentions, 'When an individual loves another for the sake of Almighty Allah, in reality it is Allah who is loved, for whenever you think of your beloved in your heart and the love is for the sake of Almighty Allah, then it is Almighty Allah whom you are actually loving and due to this reason, your love for Allah will increase. For example, when you remember and think of the Prophets, Companions and the pious people, this contemplation over them will lead you to the love of Almighty Allah who in reality bestowed these pious people with those favours (due to which you love them)'.[129]

Imam ibn al-Qayyim RA mentions, 'Love is the life of the human heart and the nourishment of the souls (when an individual's heart loves, that is when it is truly satisfied, therefore, one should love Almighty Allah, the Prophet ﷺ and the pious), the heart has no life, pleasure, satisfaction or even success except with the love. When the heart fails to love, then it suffers extreme pain and agony; an agony beyond that which the eye can see, the ear can hear, the nose can smell, the tongue can speak of. Rather, if the heart is devoid of the love of Almighty Allah, then its destruction is worse than a being without a soul'.[130]

Ibn Qudamah al-Maqdisi RA mentions, 'The sign of divine love (i.e. the sign that an individual loves Almighty Allah and His commands) is that the lover gains an unparalleled satisfaction and solace whilst secretly conversing with the beloved. The individual who reaches a state of absolute divine love also feels blessed by loneliness (as he loves being lost in thoughts of the beloved, he neither needs nor seeks the presence of others). Furthermore, the person in love feels disheartened by anything which distracts his seclusion (with the beloved). When this love intensifies,

---

[126] Al-Ikhwaan by Ibn Abu ad-Dunya vol 1 page 248.
[127] See narration number 13 in Saheeh al-Bukhari.
[128] Al-Lami' as-Sabeeh by Shams ad-Din al-Birmawi, vol 17 page 219.
[129] Majmu' al-Fatawa by Ibn Taymiyyah, vol 10 page 608.
[130] Al-Jawab al-Kafi by Ibn al-Qayyim

seclusion becomes the coolness of his eyes and removes all his pains and worries; furthermore, the love overpowers his heart to such an extent that he becomes completely detached from the world (and completely connected with the beloved - Almighty Allah)'.[131]

However, it is important to understand that this love comes after constant striving and effort. Imam Thaabit al-Bunaani RA mentioned, 'I struggled (by staying determined against my desires whilst) performing the prayer for twenty years, only after that, I enjoyed (and gained pleasure) performing the prayer for twenty years'.[132]

[131] Mukhtasar Minhaj al-Qasideen by Ibn Qudamah, vol 4 page 117.
[132] Siyar A'lam an-Nubala, vol 9 page 258.

لَا يَرْحَمُ اللهُ مَنْ لَا يَرْحَمُ النَّاسَ

Allah will not shower mercy upon the individual who does not show mercy to mankind

(Sahih al-Bukhari)

Mercy, love and kindness are the characters of the Prophets and the pious folk, Almighty Allah has made mention, 'So, it is through the mercy from Allah that you (Oh Muhammad ﷺ) were lenient with them (i.e. with the people around you). If you had been rude (in speech) and harsh of heart, they would have abandoned you'.[133]

Mercy is an immediate characteristic of Almighty Allah and He Himself is the most merciful. Certain captives were once taken in a war and brought before the Prophet ﷺ, there was a woman amongst them and whenever she passed a child amongst the captives, she took the child towards her chest and nursed it. The Prophet ﷺ asked the Companions, 'Do you think this mother would ever throw her own child in the fire (when she is so loving that she is even caring for the children of others)?' The Companions replied that she will never allow her child to be thrown in the fire. Upon hearing this response, the Prophet ﷺ mentioned, 'Almighty Allah is even more merciful than this lady is towards her child'.[134]

Almighty Allah is ever-ready to shower His mercy upon us and forgive our countless sins and save us from the fire of Hell, however, it is in our best interest to strive towards the fulfilment of the commands of Almighty Allah, the essence of this is beautifully demonstrated in a narration wherein the Prophet ﷺ informs us, 'When Allah created the creation, He wrote in His book - and this book is placed with Him on the Throne - regarding Himself, 'My Mercy prevails over My anger'.[135] This is clearly indicative of the immense quantity and inclusive nature of the mercy of Almighty Allah.[136] Nevertheless, this mercy is reserved only for those individuals who adopt the correct beliefs and methodology, yet occasionally erred; for them there is great hope in the mercy of Allah that He will forgive the majority of (and hopefully all of) their sins and enter them into Paradise.[137]

---

[133] Surah 'Ali 'Imran, ayah 159.
[134] Saheeh al-Bukhari, hadeeth number 5999.
[135] Saheeh al-Bukhari, hadeeth number 7404.
[136] Ad-Dibaaj 'Ala Muslim, vol 6 page 97.
[137] See: Hashiyah as-Sindi 'Ala Ibn Majah, vol 8, page 146.

Mulla 'Ali al-Qari RA has been quoted to have said, 'The mercy of Almighty Allah is inclusive for believers and non-believers alike (in this world), rather the mercy of Allah is inclusive to all of his creation'.[138]

This quality of mercy is clearly visible throughout the life of the Prophet ﷺ and is rife with numerous examples and teachings that indicate upon this. Once, a Bedouin saw the beloved Prophet ﷺ kissing a child (out of care and affection), the Bedouin surprisingly asked, 'Do you kiss your children, we never kiss them?' The Prophet ﷺ replied, 'What am I to do if mercy itself has been removed from your heart'.[139] Indeed, kissing children is a sign of mercy, if this mercy has been removed from a person's heart, then it is only Almighty Allah that can return it.[140] Therefore, one should supplicate to Allah that He place the mercy of the younger members of society in their hearts.

The Prophet ﷺ called for the mutual harmony between all believers, he mentions, 'The mutual compassion, love, and mercy amongst the believers is like an individual body, when one body part aches then the rest of the body feels that pain'.[141] In the very same manner when a single Muslim anywhere in the world is suffering, every believer should feel the pain of that individual.[142]

The Prophet ﷺ has informed us, 'Mercy is only removed from the unfortunate'.[143] Imam at-Teebi RA reasoned that one becomes merciful towards people by having softness in the heart, having softness in the heart is a sign of faith, if an individual does not have softness in their heart, then they are deprived of faith, and the one who has been deprived from faith is truly unfortunate.[144]

The Prophet ﷺ mentioned, 'The individual who fails to show mercy upon the youth and fails to respect the elderly is not from amongst the believers'.[145]

'Umar ibn 'Abd al-'Aziz RA mentioned, 'Oh Allah, if I am not worthy of reaching Your mercy, indeed, Your mercy is worthy of reaching me. Verily, Your mercy encompasses everything and I am also a thing'.[146]

Sufyan ibn 'Uyaynah RA mentioned, 'Hellfire has been created as a mercy by Almighty Allah, the servants are driven away from evil out of fear of the fire'.[147] In

---

[138] Mirqaat al-Mafateeh, vol 9 page 3634. Also see: Al-Kawkab al-Wahhaj, vol 25 page 203.
[139] Saheeh al-Bukhari, narration number 5998.
[140] Al-Mafateeh by az-Zaydani, vol 5 page 213.
[141] Saheeh al-Bukhari, hadeeth number 6011.
[142] Al-Kawthar al-Jari by Ahmad al-Kurani, vol 9 page 419.
[143] Sunan Abu Dawood, hadeeth number 4944.
[144] Al-Kashif, vol 10 page 3184.
[145] Sunan at-Tirmidhi, vol 3 page 208, Hadeeth number 2033.
[146] Hilyah al-Awliya'.

essence, Hellfire serves as a deterrent for us from doing any evil and wrongdoing; indeed this is a great mercy from Almighty Allah as us weak humans without any deterrents would waste our lives in evil rather than good and productivity.

---

[147] Hilyah al-Awliya'.

تُطْعِمُ الطَّعَامَ وَتَقْرَأُ السَّلَامَ عَلَى مَنْ عَرَفْتَ وَمَنْ لَمْ تَعْرِفْ

Feed the poor and spread Salaam to those whom you know and those whom you do not know

(Sahih al-Bukhari)

The Prophet ﷺ was asked regarding which form of Islam was the best and so he ﷺ replied, 'Feeding people and spreading peace *(salaam)* to everyone, whether you know them or you don't know them'.[148] Imam Bukhari RA mentions this narration and then emphasises that feeding people (with lofty intentions) is also an integral part of Islamic teachings.

'Allamah al-'Ayni RA explains that the Arabic word used for feeding people includes food and drink, so whether an individual feeds another or they quench the thirst of another, they will receive the rewards indicated towards in this narration. He adds that this narration includes all forms of hospitality, the feeding of the poor (whether that includes bringing them to your home or sending food for them or even giving them the money to buy food). 'Allamah al-'Ayni RA further adds that the feeding is not restricted to Muslims, rather it extends to non-Muslims, even animals; so if an individual feeds non-Muslims or animals, then they will be rewarded abundantly. In fact, even if it was obligatory feeding that one did (as part of Zakah or expiation) or voluntary feeding, in both cases the extra reward of 'feeding' will be acquired.[149]

In the above narration, the Prophet ﷺ made mention of two deeds which were understood to be the best aspects of religion, a number of scholars mention that one of the aforementioned deeds (feeding others) is a monetary deed, whereas, the other (spreading greetings and peace) is a physical deed, the Prophet ﷺ has indirectly indicated towards the importance of both monetary deeds along with physical deeds.[150]

Some scholars have reasoned that the Prophet ﷺ mentioned these two deeds specifically because they were the need of the time, a number of scholars indicate this narration was revealed soon after the migration to Madinah, the Prophet ﷺ is

[148] Saheeh al-Bukhari, narration number 12.
[149] 'Umdah al-Qari by al-'Ayni, vol 1 page 368-370.
[150] 'Umdah al-Qari by al-'Ayni, vol 1 page 370.

encouraging the residents of Madinah to feed others and to specifically take care of the travellers from Makkah and also to show hospitality towards them.[151]

Ibn Rajab al-Hanbali RA mentioned that by merely feeding others one can attain Paradise and achieve emancipation from Hellfire because Almighty Allah mentioned in the Qur'an, 'But he has made no effort to cross the path that is steep. And what will make you aware of the path that is steep? (One can cross the steep and difficult path by) Freeing a slave or feeding an individual at a time of severe hunger (and famine), feeding a related orphan or a severely poor person'.[152]

Ibn Rajab al-Hanbali RA mentioned that many pious individuals would not eat unless they had a guest eating with them.[153]

It is reported regarding the great Companion, Ibn 'Umar ﵄ that he never used to break his fast except with an orphan or a poor person.[154]

Imam al-Baaji RA mentions, 'It was possibly due to this narration of feeding and greeting that 'Abdullah ibn 'Umar ﵄ used to set off in the morning towards the market places, not with the intention of purchasing any stock or produce, rather it was just to meet the people and to spread *salaam* (peace and greetings)'.[155]

However, al-Baaji RA adds that this act of 'Abdullah ibn 'Umar ﵄ is a worthy deed so long as an individual can warn against any immoral acts that may occur in the market place, if one cannot stop (or at least attempt to stop) any immoral acts, then for that individual remaining in the safety of the home is better.[156]

---

[151] 'Umdah al-Qari by al-'Ayni, vol 1 page 370.
[152] Surah al-Balad, surah 90, verses 11-16.
[153] Ikhtiyaar al-Uwla fi Sharh Hadeeth akhtisaam al-Mala' al-a'la, vol 1 page 10.
[154] Ikhtiyaar al-Uwla fi Sharh Hadeeth akhtisaam al-Mala' al-a'la, vol 1 page 10.
[155] Al-Muntaqa' by al-Baji, vol 4 page 398.
[156] Al-Muntaqa' by al-Baji, vol 4 page 398.

مَا كَانَ ضَحِكُ رَسُوْلُ اللهِ صَلَى اللهُ عَلَيْهِ وَسَلَّمَ إِلَّا تَبَسُّمًا

The Messenger of Allah ﷺ would not laugh aloud, rather he would smile

(Sahih at-Tirmidhi)

Islam guides an individual in regard to every aspect of their life, this also includes how an individual should smile and laugh. The Prophet ﷺ would frequently smile and would encounter people with a cheerful and glowing face. However, he would not laugh to the extent that a noise could be heard and rarely would his teeth be exposed whilst smiling, although there are a few narrations which suggest that there were moments when the Prophet ﷺ smiled in such a way that his teeth were exposed, however, they are a very rare occurrence and not the frequent habit of the Prophet ﷺ.[157]

A few narrations also indicate that his smile was such that his molar teeth would be made visible when smiling, however, a large number of scholars have explained this away as either an extremely rare occurrence (indicating to the extreme joy or good news), or merely an exaggeration on the part of the narrator (to demonstrate the level of happiness), others translate the word 'laughter' as excessively smiling.[158]

In conclusion, one can infer from the commentary of the scholars that the Prophet ﷺ was extremely cheerful and constantly smiling, whereas laughter with noise or such laughter wherein the molars would be shown was a rarity. This is further strengthened by the narration of 'Abdullah ibn al-Harith رضي الله عنه who mentions, 'I have not seen anyone smile more than the Prophet ﷺ.[159]

The Prophet ﷺ gave some extremely crucial pieces of advice to Abu Hurairah رضي الله عنه, he enquired, 'Who will take these statements from me, so that they may act upon them or teach them to someone else who may act upon them?' Abu Hurairah رضي الله عنه narrates, 'I said, "I shall, Oh Messenger of Allah!" So the Prophet ﷺ took my hand and counted five (things), he said, "[1] Beware of the unlawful and you shall be the greatest worshipper from amongst the people, [2] be satisfied with what Allah has decreed for you and you shall be the richest of the people, [3] be kind to your neighbour and you shall be a believer, [4] love for the people what you love for

[157] Tuhfah al-Ahwadhi, vol 9 page 51.
[158] Jam' al-Wasa'il by 'Ali al-Qari.
[159] Sunan at-Tirmidhi, vol 5 page 24, Hadeeth number 3942.

yourself and you shall be a Muslim [5] and do not laugh much, for indeed excessive laughter kills the heart".[160]

Imam Muhammad as-San'aani RA reasons as to why excessive laughter is a means of killing the heart, he writes, 'Excessive laughter creates a joy and inclination towards the world (thus making a person further indulge in the world), whereas, the life (and eternal comfort) of the heart is in its distance from this world (and its love) towards the worship and remembrance of Almighty Allah (and preparing for the eternal life of the hereafter)'.[161]

Imam Ghazaali RA indicates that excessive laughter can sometimes create hatred, it decreases reverence and dignity.[162]

Hafidh al-Munaawi RA comments that excessive laughter covers the heart in darkness, it becomes like the deceased individual who can neither benefit themselves in any manner nor can they remove any harm from themselves.[163]

The Prophet ﷺ whilst advising the Companions once said, 'If you (Companions) knew that which I know, then you would laugh very little and weep much more'.[164]

Some scholars have explained this narration in the following manner, 'If you (Companions) knew that which I know in regards to the hereafter; the rewards and its punishments, then you would laugh very little afraid of the punishment and remorse at not attaining the encompassing mercy of Almighty Allah and weep excessively out of fear of the hereafter or over ones wrongdoings'.[165]

We pray Almighty Allah allows us to maintain the Prophetic balance, being cheerful and happy in moderation, without being neglectful of the eternal life, the hereafter.

---

[160] Sunan at-Tirmidhi, vol 3 page 403, Hadeeth number 2460.
[161] At-Tanwir Sharh al-Jami' as-Sagheer by Imam as-San'ani, vol 8 page 241.
[162] Ihya 'Uloom ad-Din, vol 3 page 128.
[163] At-Tayseer Bi Sharh al-Jami' as-Sagheer, vol 1 page 53.
[164] Saheeh al-Bukhari, hadeeth number 1044.
[165] See Kawthar al-Mani' ad-Darari ot Muhammad as-Shanqitee, vol 10 page 403-404.

لَا يَنْبَغِيْ لِصِدِّيْقٍ أَنْ يَكُوْنَ لَعَّانًا

It is not appropriate for a truthful person that he be one to invoke curses

(Sahih Muslim)

Invoking curses upon others and failing to control one's tongue is greatly disliked in the religion and regarded as a sin. Almighty Allah mentions, 'Allah does not like the public mention of evil except by the one who has been wronged. And Allah is All-Hearing and All-Knowing'.[166]

Doctor Wahbah RA mentions in the commentary of this verse, 'Safeguarding the tongue from filth and the speaking of good is from the mannerisms of a strong believer. A believer should never be one who curses or involves himself in accusing and swearing at others, nor should they harm others with any other form of abuse. Whenever an individual controls their tongue and refrains from speaking unnecessarily it will be from their wisdom and intelligence, they will have little to regret from the statements uttered from their tongues nor will they ever need to provide excuses and cover-ups; and forever they will be regarded as noble individuals and people of dignity'.[167] He then adds, 'One of the purposes of religion is to encourage people to spread a good word and refrain from evil talk'.

The Prophet ﷺ mentioned, 'Modesty is a part of faith and faith will be in Paradise (i.e. whoever will hold onto modesty will follow it into Paradise). Rude (and offensive) speech is a construct of harshness and harshness will be in Hell (i.e. will lead to Hell)'.[168]

The Prophet ﷺ mentioned, 'A believer does not dishonour (anyone), nor does he curse (any individual) and nor is he immoral or shameless (in his words and actions, etc.)'.[169]

Ibn 'Umar ﷺ mentioned, 'The most disliked people to Almighty Allah are those who invoke abuse and curse at others'.[170]

---

[166] Surah an-Nisa', 4:148.

[167] At-Tafseer al-Waseet, vol 1 page 403.

[168] Sunan Ibn Majah, hadeeth number 4184. See Sharh Masabih by Ibn al-Malak, vol 5 page 343.

[169] Sunan at-Tirmidhi, vol 3 page 231, Hadeeth number 2092.

[170] Ihya 'Ulum ad-Din, vol 3 page 126.

The Prophet ﷺ mentioned, 'To invoke curses upon a believer is tantamount to killing him'.[171] In exactly the same way the murder of a believer is totally forbidden and stands as a major sin, the cursing of a believer (taunting him and speaking evil regarding him) is also forbidden to a similar degree.[172]

Imam ibn Daqeeq al-'Eed RA writes that the cursing of an individual refers to supplicating that the individual be deprived from the mercy of Almighty Allah. Thereafter he adds, 'When an individual curses another and the prayer is accepted such that the individual (who was prayed against) is deprived of the mercy of Almighty Allah, then this is extremely harmful for any person; more so than even killing them, for killing an individual merely removes them from this temporary world, whereas, praying for the deprivation from mercy has the potential to result in numerous harms and difficulties (and as a result of which one may be deprived from the eternal mercy of Almighty Allah in this temporary abode and also the hereafter)'.[173]

---

[171] Saheeh al-Bukhari, hadeeth number 6105.
[172] Hashiyah as-Sindi for Saheeh al-Bukhari, vol 4 page 69.
[173] Ihkam al-Ahkam, vol 1 page 461.

مَنْ لَمْ يَشْكُرِ النَّاسَ لَمْ يَشْكُرِ اللهَ

One who is not grateful to people, is not grateful to Allah

(Sunan at-Tirmdhi)

Whenever a favour is bestowed upon an individual, it is a test from Almighty Allah. Just as an individual is tested through hardships and difficulties, Almighty Allah sometimes tests us with prosperity and bounties. Almighty Allah desires to see our reactions in both scenarios; whether the moments of ease and affluence or the moments of trials and difficulty, it is from the excellence of an individual's faith that we always turn in patience and gratitude to Almighty Allah alone.

Almighty Allah mentions, 'If you show gratitude, I will surely increase you [in favours], but if you deny, indeed, My punishment is severe'.[174]

The great scholar, Sufyaan ath-Thawri RA indicates in the commentary of this verse, 'If we show gratitude to Allah in regard to His innumerable favours upon us, then Almighty Allah will increase our ability to worship Him (thus accruing more reward for the hereafter and increasing in the pleasure of Almighty Allah)'.[175]

The fourth Caliph, Ali ﷺ once mentioned, 'Favours are correlatively connected with gratitude, the showing of gratitude will always increase the blessings from Almighty Allah, the blessings of Almighty Allah do not stop until the gratitude and thanks from the servant does not stop'.[176]

The pious were once asked regarding the meaning of *shukr* (showing gratitude), they replied, 'One should not become courageous upon the continual performance of sins despite knowing the innumerous bounties of Almighty Allah upon you!'[177]

The judge, ibn 'Arabi RA simply defined gratitude as, 'To use the bounties of Allah in acts of obedience', he then summarised ingratitude as, 'using those very bounties in acts of disobedience'.[178]

'Abu 'Abdurrahman al-Hubali RA mentioned, 'Prayer is a form of gratitude, fasting is a form of gratitude, every good deed a person does for the pleasure of Almighty Allah is a form of gratitude, the best form of gratitude is to praise Almighty Allah'.[179]

---

174 Surah 'Ibrahim, 14:7.
175 Tafseer Ibn Abi Hatim.
176 Uddah as-Sabireen, chapter 22 page 10.
177 Tafseer al-Mawardi, vol 3 page 123.
178 Ahkam al-Qur'an, vol 6 page 462.

Scholars indicate that the best form of gratitude after using the bounties in the correct prescribed manner (in acts of goodness) is to understand, appreciate and accept that the favours of Almighty Allah are in such abundance that one can never even come close to showing enough gratitude. Prophet Dawud عليه السلام asked Almighty Allah, 'Oh Lord, how can I show gratitude to Yourself? Indeed my showing of gratitude is itself another bounty from Yourself!' The response from the Almighty upon this was, 'Oh Dawud, now you have truly shown gratitude'.[180]

From the above, the importance of showing gratitude to Almighty Allah upon His blessings and favours is understood. However, gratitude is not limited to the being of Almighty Allah, if any from amongst the creation of Almighty Allah renders a favour upon you, then one should show gratitude towards them and thank them too.

The Prophet ﷺ mentioned, 'If a favour is rendered upon an individual and they thank the one who bestowed the favour with the words, "May Allah reward you with the best of reward"[181], then he has fulfilled the rights of that good to the best of his ability'.[182] Scholars explain that supplicating to the Almighty Allah for an individual who has favoured you is definitely a worthy expiation, for who can reward better than Almighty Allah![183]

Fudhayl ibn 'Iyadh RA mentioned, 'Hold firm to the showing of gratitude, for when the favours are taken away from the people (due to a lack of gratitude shown), very rarely do they return'.[184]

As the pious would say, 'Blessings are like wild animals, tame them by showing gratitude'.[185]

Hence, we should make it a habit to thank Almighty Allah along with those who have showed any favour upon us; small or big, the more thanks and gratitude we show, the more favours Almighty Allah will bestow us with.

---

[179] Al-Hidayah Ila an-Nihayah, vol 9 page 5901.
[180] Tafseer as-Sulami, vol 1 page 341.
[181] جَزَاكَ اللّٰهُ خَيْرًا
[182] Sunan at-Tirmidhi, vol 3 page 254, Hadeeth number 2154.
[183] Al-Badr at-Tamam Sharh Bulugh al-Maram, vol 9 page 486.
[184] Ihya 'Ulum ad-Din, vol 4 page 127.
[185] Ihya 'Ulum ad-Din, vol 4 page 127.

خَالِقِ النَّاسَ بِخُلُقٍ حَسَنٍ

Show lofty manners to all people

(Sunan at-Tirmdhi)

One of the primary objectives in sending Prophet Muhammad ﷺ to this world was to educate and perfect virtuous character.[186]

Abu ‘Amr al-Qurtubi RA mentioned, ‘The perfection of virtuous character includes piety, all types of goodness, religiosity, dignified deeds, favours to others, justice (at all times); indeed, the Prophet Muhammad ﷺ came to perfect all of these ideas’.[187]

Abu al-Waleed al-Baaji RA mentions that Arabs were the people with the best of manners even prior to the advent of the Prophet Muhammad ﷺ, however due to some of the evils they were committing, a number of imperfections had seeped into their character which tainted their reputation. Therefore, Prophet Muhammad ﷺ was sent with Islam (monotheism) which corrected the shortcomings within the mannerisms of the Arabs.[188]

From the etiquette of perfecting one’s manners is to ask Almighty Allah to beautify oneself with the best of manners. The Prophet ﷺ would supplicate to Almighty Allah, ‘Oh Allah, guide me to the best of character, for no one can guide to the best of character except You. Oh Allah, protect me from unpleasant character, for no one can protect from unpleasant character except You’.[189] Imam al-Qurtubi RA has mentioned that this supplication could either be a request to beautify an individual with noble traits and distance them from any evil qualities, it could also have the meaning, ‘Oh Allah, grant me the ability to fulfil your commands and forgive my shortcomings (as no conduct is perfect except that which is in accordance to Your commands and teachings)’.[190]

The Prophet ﷺ would oft supplicate to Almighty Allah for the improvement and rectification of his character despite Almighty Allah having stated in the Qur’an, ‘And indeed, you are of great moral character’.[191]

---

[186] Musnad Ahmad, Hadeeth number 8952.
[187] At-Tamheed, vol 24 page 334.
[188] Al-Muntaqa’, vol 4 page 292.
[189] Saheeh Muslim, Hadeeth Number 1848.
[190] Al-Mufhim, vol 7 page 35.
[191] Surah al-Qalam, verse 4.

Mulla ‘Ali al-Qari RA mentions, ‘The Prophet ﷺ was beseeching Allah to further improve his character despite his current exemplary character’.[192] This demonstrates the importance of lofty morals and character, despite the Prophet ﷺ already being adorned with the best of character, he further wanted to improve his character.

The character of the Prophet ﷺ was such that a slave-girl from Madinah would feel no hesitation to take him by his hand and lead him wherever she needed (to assist with some work).[193] The Prophet ﷺ could easily have refused to be taken in this manner by a mere slave-girl, as after all, he was an extremely well respected leader of Madinah. However, the Prophet ﷺ humbled himself in order to fulfil her needs - this was to set a perfect precedent for his followers.

Some scholars have defined good character as the individual who is at peace with himself and the people are also at peace with him.[194] This would include being at peace with all the creation of Almighty Allah, whether humans or non-humans, whether Muslim or non-Muslim, for only then can one truly be qualified to be labelled as one having good character.

A number of scholars would mention that if one is adorned with good character, the doors of wealth and sustenance will be thrown open for them.[195]

---

[192] Jam’ al-Wasail by Mulla ‘Ali al-Qari.
[193] Saheeh al-Bukhari, Hadeeth number 6072.
[194] Adab ad-Dunya’ wad-Din, vol 1 page 299.
[195] Adab ad-Dunya’ wad-Din, vol 1 page 299.

مَا تَوَاضَعَ أَحَدٌ لِلّٰهِ إِلَّا رَفَعَهُ اللّٰهُ

None have ever humbled themselves for the sake of Allah, except that Allah has elevated them

(Sahih Muslim)

Humility is a quality that has been at the fore of our religion, the Prophet ﷺ advised his Companions to be humble in their interactions with all of humanity, he ﷺ also set the stellar standard of humility. He also taught that humility is a quality that should specifically be employed towards one senior in age, knowledge and in leadership. Rather, the religion of Islam even encourages one to be humble towards the youth, the Prophet ﷺ was humble even to very young children.

The Prophet ﷺ stood to give a sermon once when he mentioned, 'Allah has revealed upon me that we should be humble to one another, none of us should show pride (and arrogance) and no person should oppress another'.[196]

In this narration three very clear messages have been provided as an instruction from Almighty Allah, [1] to show humility towards all, [2] to avoid pride against all, [3] to avoid oppression of all. No doubt, the life of our beloved Prophet ﷺ practically demonstrates all of these characteristics to an exemplary standard.

Anas ibn Malik رضي الله عنه mentions, 'The Prophet ﷺ would pass by children and greet them with love (and warmth)'.[197]

Imam Nawawi RA comments, 'This narration indicates to... the virtue of humility, spreading greetings to all, it also highlights the humility of the Prophet ﷺ and his mercy towards all of mankind'.[198]

Imam Abu al-Hasan ibn Battal RA enumerates multiple benefits of greeting children, he mentions, 'One of the signs of exemplary character in the Prophet ﷺ was his greeting the youth, it demonstrates his sublime manners and his humility, for it was a form of training for the children to practically replicate the lifestyle of the Prophet ﷺ and adopt similar manners from their early infancy, such that when they reach puberty, they are accustomed to these blessed practices'. Ibn Battal RA adds, 'The Prophet ﷺ would play (and spend quality time) with children so that his followers

---

[196] Saheeh Muslim, Hadeeth number 7389.
[197] Saheeh Muslim, Hadeeth number 5791.
[198] Al-Minhaj, vol 7 page 302.

would also learn from his example. Indeed, the Prophet ﷺ never did anything, even if it was assumed to be a minor act, except that it was to be adopted as a lifestyle to be followed by Muslims to come; even in his playing with children, the Prophet ﷺ was training his soul (and by extension guiding others to train their souls) to being humble and crushing one's pride'.[199]

The Prophet ﷺ warned us, 'No individual who has pride in their heart equal to the weight of a grain of a mustard seed can enter paradise'.[200]

Imam Khattaabi RA explains this narration further, 'Some forms of pride are such that they prevent an individual from entering Paradise forever, whereas, other forms are such that after an individual is cleansed from it, they can enter Paradise purified from any form of pride."[201]

These narrations clearly highlight that humility is necessary for one's entrance into Paradise; that explains why it was labelled as the best of worships. Our beloved mother, 'Aisha RA warned, 'You people are careless regarding the best form of worship, humility'.[202]

The great saint, Hasan al-Basri RA was asked regarding humbleness, he replied, "Humbleness is such that when a person leaves his house and meets any Muslim (on the streets, etc.), he thinks of them to have virtue over him."[203] Hasan al-Basri regarded humbleness is when a person thinks of everyone around you as to have an honour and virtue over yourself; irrespective of their age.

A similar definition of humbleness was given by the saint, al-Fudhayl RA, he defined humility thus, 'You submit to the truth even if you hear it from a child, or even if you hear it from the most ignorant of people, you still accept the truth'.[204]

The great scholar, 'Abdullah ibn al-Mubarak رحمه الله mentioned, 'The peak of humility is that you compare yourself to the individual who has less than you in this world and you do not think of yourself as more virtuous than them due to your worldly success, then, you compare yourself with an individual who has more than you in this world and you do not think of him as more virtuous than yourself due to his worldly success'.[205] According to 'Abdullah ibn Mubarak رحمه الله, the essence of humility

[199] Sharh Saheeh al-Bukhari by Ibn Battal, vol 9 page 27.
[200] Sunan Abu Dawood, Hadeeth number 4091.
[201] Ma'lim as-Sunan, vol 4 page 196.
[202] Sunan an-Nasai', Hadeeth number 11852.
[203] Az-Zawajir 'An Iqtiraaf al-Kabair by Ibn Hajar al-Makki, vol 1 page 196.
[204] Hilyah al-Awliyaa, vol 8 page 91.
[205] At-Tawadu' wal-Kumool by Ibn Abi ad-Dunya, vol 1 page 119.

is to turn one's attention away from this world towards the obedience of Almighty Allah and the successes of the hereafter.

Ibrahim ibn Shayban RA eloquently pronounced, 'Dignity is hidden in humility, honour is hidden in god-consciousness and freedom is hidden in contentment'.[206]

---

[206] Ar-Risalah al-Qushayriyyah, vol 1 page 69.

إِيَّاكُمْ وَالظَّنَّ فَإِنَّ الظَّنَّ أَكْذَبُ الْحَدِيْثِ

Beware of suspicion, for suspicion is the worst form of false speech

(Sahih al-Bukhari)

Islam forbids the application of blanket suspicions and accusing anybody with false labels and ungrounded assumptions without any valid proof and evidence. Further, in matters of suspecting another's intentions, one should accept what the others are verbalising and leave their internal matters and thoughts to Almighty Allah, for indeed He is aware of what thoughts cross the hearts.

Almighty Allah mentions, 'Oh believers, avoid suspicion (and negative assumptions), indeed, some suspicions are sinful'.[207]

The Companion, 'Abdullah Ibn 'Abbas ﷺ mentions in the commentary of this verse, 'Almighty Allah prohibits Muslims from holding any negative assumptions regarding others'.[208]

A number of scholars have clarified that all forms of negative assumptions and suspicions are prohibited, however, positive thoughts and assumptions are permitted, rather advised. Imam at-Tabari RA makes mentions, 'In the above verse, only a very few types of assumptions were deemed as sinful, the reason for this is because believers are permitted to have lofty and positive thoughts of others (and should always give others the benefit of the doubt). For indeed Almighty Allah mentions, 'Why, when you heard regarding it (the slander and accusation of adultery), did the believing men and believing women not think positively of one another and say, "This is an obvious falsehood?"'[209] This verse proves that good assumptions (and giving others the benefit of the doubt) is actually from good character, therefore, only negative assumptions and suspicions are forbidden'.[210]

The Companion, Mu'adh ibn Jabal ﷺ once led the people in prayer and recited the chapter of *al-Baqarah* (the second chapter of the Qur'an), an individual who was praying behind him left the row and offered a shorter prayer separately and then went away. When Mu'adh ﷺ was informed of this incident, he claimed that this specific individual was a hypocrite (based on him praying a shorter prayer and leaving). Later, when the man heard of this statement that was made regarding him

[207] Surah al-Hujura, verse 12.
[208] Shu'ab al-Iman by Imam al-Bayhaqi, Narration number 6330.
[209] Surah an-Nur, verse 12.
[210] Tafseer at-Tabari, vol 21 page 373.

by Mu'adh ﷺ, he immediately came to the Prophet ﷺ and mentioned the incident to him and complained regarding what Mu'adh ﷺ had mentioned, he also added that he (tirelessly) works throughout the day and a lengthy night prayer is too difficult upon him. The Prophet ﷺ called for Mu'adh ﷺ and rebuked him by saying, 'Oh Mu'adh, you are putting people through trials (and trouble)!' Thereafter, he advised Mu'adh ﷺ to recite considerably shorter portions from the Qur'an.[211] Scholars have indicated towards this narration and mentioned that the Prophet ﷺ rebuked Mu'adh ﷺ thrice upon his statement, this serves as a lesson to all who would follow that one should not be hasty in jumping to conclusions nor should they formulate ungrounded assumptions without having complete knowledge of an individual's context and circumstances.

Scholars have further emphasised that one should not even harbour negative and despondent thoughts regarding Almighty Allah, (i.e. whether the help of Almighty Allah will come or not). One should never feel that Almighty Allah will not forgive their sins, rather they should turn to Almighty Allah in hope and confidence that they will be forgiven. Once the scholar 'Abdullah ibn Mubarak ﷺ came to Sufyan ﷺ during the pilgrimage on the plain of 'Arafah, Sufyan ﷺ was knelt on his knees weeping profusely, 'Abdullah ﷺ mentions that he too began to cry, Sufyan ﷺ then turned to face him and enquired as to what had happened, so Abdullah ﷺ responded, 'At this very moment in time, who is the worst person to be gathered in this plain of 'Arafah? Sufyan ﷺ replied, 'The individual who thinks Almighty Allah will not forgive him!'[212]

[211] The complete narration is in Saheeh al-Bukhari, Hadeeth number 6106.
[212] Husn ad-Dhann bi-Allah by Ibn Abi Dunya, narration 78.

لَا تَحَسَّسُوْا وَلَا تَجَسَّسُوْا وَلَا تَحَاسَدُوْا وَلَا تَدَابَرُوْا وَلَا تَبَاغَضُوْا

Do not eavesdrop, do not spy, do not be jealous of one another nor cut relations with one another and do not hate one another

(Sahih al-Bukhari)

The Qur'an and the Prophetic traditions have always stressed the importance of good etiquette in all aspects of an individual's life, this includes the forbidding of spying on others, harbouring jealousy and being (negatively) envious of others; Islam has greatly despised the cutting of ties with others and having hatred for others.

Abu Hurairah ﵁ narrates that the Messenger of Allah ﷺ said, 'Beware of suspicion, for verily suspicion is from the worst of false speech, make sure not to search for the faults that lie in others, not to spy on one another and neither be jealous of one another, do not desert (cut your relations with) one another and do not harbour hatred for one another, Oh slaves of Allah, be brothers unto one another!'[213]

Sufyan ath-Thawri RA mentions, 'The assumptions that are made can be divided into two; those which lead to sin and those that do not lead to sin. The assumptions for which one is sinful are those which he verbalises, whereas, those that are not verbalised and remain as mere thoughts will not result in sin (rather, these assumptions only cross an individual's mind and are shunned)'.[214]

Mu'awiyah RA mentions regarding jealousy, 'No bad habit is worse than jealousy, the jealous individual will die before they reach the person (or thing) which they were jealous of'.[215]

A Bedouin beautifully presented the reality of jealousy; he states, 'I have never seen an oppressor who resembles the oppressed individual more than the jealous, for, every blessing they see with you, they suffer pain'.[216]

Abu Darda' ﵁ mentioned the cure of jealousy, he mentioned, 'If an individual increases their remembrance of death, then their desires and jealousy will decrease'.[217]

---

[213] Saheeh al-Bukhari, hadeeth number 6064.
[214] Al-Istizkaar, vol 9 page 269.
[215] Adab ad-Dunya' wad-Din, vol 1 page 334.
[216] Ihya 'Ulum ad-Din, vol 3 page 189.
[217] Az-Zawajir by Ibn Hajar al-Haytami, vol 1 page 143.

Islam has reminded time and again the great value of upholding the ties of familial relationships, Abu Hurairah ﵁ narrated that the Messenger of Allah ﷺ said, 'The gates of Paradise are thrown open on Mondays and Thursdays, any servant (of Allah) who does not associate any partners with Him shall be forgiven (on these days), except for the man who bears a grudge with his brother, it is then announced (to the angels), "Delay (the forgiveness of) these two individuals until they reconcile; delay these two until they reconcile; delay these two until they reconcile"'.[218]

Once, al-Hasan ﵁ and al-Husayn ﵁, the sons of 'Ali ﵁ were involved in a dispute which led to a separation between them wherein they stopped talking to each other. However, after three days, al-Hasan ﵁ went to al-Husayn ﵁ whilst he was sat and al-Hasan ﵁ kissed his younger brother, al-Husayn ﵁ on the forehead (clarifying that any animosity between them was only short-lived). Al-Husayn ﵁ later mentioned that he had seriously considered making up with al-Hasan ﵁ earlier and clearing up the air, however, the only reason he never reconciled first was because the elder brother, al-Hasan ﵁ was more worthy of the honour that comes with initiating the reconciliation, al-Husayn ﵁ disliked taking this honour away from his elder brother'.[219]

---

[218] Saheeh Muslim, hadeeth number 6709.

[219] Masawi' al-Akhlaaq by al-Kharaiti, narration number 536.

كُوْنُوْا عِبَادَ اللهِ إِخْوَانًا

Oh slaves of Allah! Be brothers unto one another

(Sahih al-Bukhari)

Brotherhood and unity has always been a fundamental foundation within the Islamic teachings, numerous prophetic narrations have laid an emphasis in regard to the harmony, love and affection an individual should maintain for others.

Almighty Allah mentions in the Qur'an, 'The believers are brothers (and a family), so you should reconcile between your brothers (in the occurrence of any dispute), fear Almighty Allah (in all matters), and there is hope you shall be showered with mercy'.[220]

Imam al-Qurtubi RA explains in the commentary of this verse, 'The bond of brotherhood based on religious motives (amongst the believers) is stronger and more deep-rooted than the brotherhood based on blood; for indeed, the brotherhood based on blood is easily broken if their religions differ (in terms of many Islamic rulings), whereas the brotherhood and bond created amongst believers is established even if one is not blood related to another'.[221]

The Prophet ﷺ greatly encouraged the helping of others, for, in our assistance of others lies the assistance of Almighty Allah; the Prophet ﷺ mentioned, 'A Muslim is the brother of another Muslim, he should neither commit oppression upon him, nor (should he) surrender him over (unjustly), and he who fulfils the need of a brother, Allah will fulfil his needs. He who relieves a Muslim from hardship, Allah will relieve him from the hardships of the Day of Judgement. He who does not expose (the faults of another Muslim), Allah will conceal him (and his faults) on the Day of Judgement'.[222]

Najm ad-Din ibn Qudamah al-Maqdisi RA comments in regard to helping a Muslim brother, 'From the assisting of another individual is the teaching of one's fellow brothers and giving good counsel to them, verily, the necessity of (increasing) knowledge is not any less than the need for wealth and money (rather, the need for

---

[220] Surah al-Hujurat, surah 49, verse 10.
[221] Tafseer al-Qurtubi, vol 16 page 322-323.
[222] Sahih al-Bukhari, hadeeth number 2442.

knowledge is greater) and so, if you are endowed with knowledge, then you should spread some of your knowledge onto your brothers in the hope of guiding them'.[223]

'Abdullah ibn Mas'ud ﵁ mentions how the Prophet's companions used to take care of each other, he narrates, 'When one of our brothers was absent for a noticeable period of time, we would go and visit him (at his home), if he was ill, then this visit would be considered as the visiting of the ill (and would result in immense rewards). If the brother was busy and engaged, we would assist him in the accomplishment of his work, and if he was away due to any other personal reason, then we would simply visit him with the intention of spending time with our brother'.[224]

Once, the Prophet ﷺ advised that a genuine indication of pure and complete faith is to 'love for one's brother that which one would love for themselves'.[225] In the very same manner that we prefer to be loved, respected and treated fairly by others, we too should lead by example by showing these very ideals to others. If we feel that we are not being treated with respect, we should deeply reflect over our own approaches and character when dealing with others, for even the mere meeting of a brother with a cheerful face holds immense reward and is considered an act of goodness in Islam.[226]

The Prophet ﷺ strongly warned against talking ill of any individual, he ﷺ once asked the Companions, 'Do you know what backbiting is?' The Companions replied, 'Allah and His Messenger ﷺ know best'. The Prophet ﷺ said, 'Backbiting is the speaking of your brother in a manner which he dislikes'. It was said to the Prophet ﷺ, 'What is your opinion if I actually find the aforementioned fault to be in my brother?' He ﷺ replied, 'If the fault is actually found in him, then, you genuinely have backbitten him, and if that fault is not found in him, then it is defined as slander'.[227]

One should supplicate for his Muslim brethren, the Prophet ﷺ mentioned, 'There is no believing servant who supplicates for his brother whilst in his absence, except that the Angels say, 'May the same be granted to you (i.e. may you also acquire that which you requested for your brother)'.[228]

A few of the wise have mentioned, 'The following acts are essential for every individual in relation to their family, [1] loving each other from the heart, [2] speaking good of one another, [3] assisting each other in moments of financial

---

[223] Mukhtasar Minhaj al-Qasideen by Ibn Qudamah, page 102.
[224] Adab al-'Ishrah by Badruddin Abu al-Barakat Muhammad al-Gazzi, page number 8.
[225] Sahih al-Bukhari, hadeeth number 13.
[226] Sahih Muslim, hadeeth number 6857.
[227] Sahih Muslim, hadeeth number 6758.
[228] Sahih Muslim, hadeeth number 7103.

difficulty, [4] assisting in (the formulation and rectification of their) good character, [5] to defend (their honour) in their absence'.[229]

[229] Al-Ikhwaan by Ibn Abu ad-Dunya, page number 111.

كَانَ رَسُوْلُ اللّٰهِ مِنْ أَحْسَنِ النَّاسِ خُلُقًا

The Prophet ﷺ was of the most impeccable character from amongst the people

(Sahih Muslim)

The Prophet ﷺ was the epitome and absolute embodiment of good character, this not only includes his interactions with near and dear but also the extended family and his treatment towards his neighbours (irrespective of faith, culture and class), his respect for the elderly and his tenderness with the youth was an exemplary display of character and the perfect lifestyle to replicate.

Once, the Prophet ﷺ sent his servant Anas ؓ for a task, Anas ؓ set off in earnest to complete the job, however, he soon got distracted by a group of friends playing and he joined in their game completely forgetting the task he set out to complete. Soon, the Prophet ﷺ himself set out to search for Anas ؓ, when he saw him playing with his friends, he approached Anas ؓ and tapped him from behind. Anas ؓ turned around to the radiant and smiling face of the Prophet ﷺ, the Prophet ﷺ calmly asked, 'Oh beloved Anas, have you completed the task?' Anas ؓ replied, 'Yes, I am going right now to complete it'.[230]

Mulla 'Ali al-Qari RA mentions regarding the character of the Prophet ﷺ, 'The Prophet ﷺ always demonstrated beautiful etiquette, unlike others whose character may falter on certain occasions'.[231]

Almighty Allah himself certified the exemplary character of the Prophet ﷺ in the Qur'an, 'Indeed you are of great stellar character'.[232]

The great saint, Junaid al-Baghdadi RA explains, 'The reason the character of the Prophet ﷺ has been declared as impeccable is because everything the Prophet ﷺ did was always for Almighty Allah (and in accordance to the commands and instructions of Almighty Allah)'.[233]

The interactions and exchanges of the Prophet ﷺ with the youth is recorded in the books of prophetic traditions. Jabir ؓ, the son of Samurah mentions, 'I performed

[230] Sahih Muslim, Hadeeth number 6155.

[231] Jam' al-Wasail by Mulla 'Ali al-Qari, chapter regarding the manners of Prophet ﷺ.

[232] Surah al-Qalam, surah number 68, verse number 4.

[233] At-Tasheel li 'Ulum at-Tanzeel by Muhammad ibn Ahmad Ibn Jizzi al-Garnati, page number 2439.

the prayer with Prophet ﷺ in the mosque, I then accompanied the Prophet ﷺ as he was returning to his family. Some young children met with the Prophet ﷺ on his way home, the Prophet ﷺ mercifully patted his hand on their cheeks, Jabir ﷺ adds that the Prophet ﷺ also patted me on my cheek from which I experienced a coolness and a fragrance from the beloved hand of the Prophet ﷺ, it was as though the hand had only just been taken out of a perfumer's scent bag'.[234]

Once, The Messenger of Allah ﷺ kissed Hasan bin 'Ali ﷺ whilst Aqra' ibn Habis at-Tameemi ﷺ was sitting beside him, Aqra' immediately said, 'I have ten children and I have never kissed any one of them'. The Messenger of Allah ﷺ glanced at him and said, 'He who is not merciful to others will not be treated mercifully (by Almighty Allah)'.[235]

These incidents indicate towards the exemplary manners and the method in which the Prophet ﷺ humbled himself when dealing with children, all of this was to spend quality time with children and give them a share of his valuable time.[236]

The Prophet ﷺ did not only care for humans, rather, he ﷺ heavily encouraged the care of animals. He once advised, 'If any Muslim plants a seed from which a human or an animal take benefit from, then they will be rewarded as though they have given that amount of charity (in the path of Almighty Allah)'.[237] Shaykh Ahmad al-Kuraani RA adds in the commentary of this narration, 'This reward extends to all forms of trees and plants grown, whether they bear fruits or not, as animals can benefit from the trees by taking shade beneath them and merely eating from their leaves'.[238]

Abu Hafs Ibn al-Mulaqqin RA comments under this (and similar narrations), 'These narrations indicate to showing mercy upon all creation, whether believers or non-believers, such that it should extend to animals too, this mercy is a means by which Almighty Allah forgives the sins of people, hence, it is appropriate for all intelligent individuals to express this mercy towards all, indeed, Almighty Allah has not created animals without a purpose'.[239]

---

[234] Sahih Muslim, Hadeeth number 6197.
[235] Sahih al-Bukhari, hadeeth number 5997.
[236] See: Al-Minhaj commentary of Sahih Muslim by Imam Nawawi, vol 8 page 40.
See: Al-Kawkab al-Wahhaj by Muhammad al-Amin al-Harari, vol 23 page 164.
[237] Sahih al-Bukhari, hadeeth number 6012.
[238] Al-Kawthar al-Jari by Ahmad ibn Isma'eel al-Kura'ni, vol 9 page 419.
[239] At-Tawdeeh by Ibn Mulaqqin, vol 28 page 315.

لَمْ يَكُنِ النَّبِيُّ فَاحِشًا وَلَا مُتَفَحِّشًا

The Prophet ﷺ was not vulgar, nor did he adopt obscene habits

(Sahih al-Bukhari)

The Prophet ﷺ was not an individual who would abuse others and he would not speak any profanities nor would he curse others. If there was ever a time when he needed to admonish somebody, he would politely ask, 'What is wrong with him?' Thereafter, he would add the customary Arabic saying, 'May his forehead be dusted!'[240]

Scholars have clarified the statement, 'May his forehead be dusted', with a number of explanations,

1. A customary proverb of the Arabs with no intended meaning.
2. A metaphor for falling on one's head due to which the forehead becomes dusted and it is used to advise an individual to study knowledge so as to remove the ignorance that made him commit the bad deed.
3. Advice to become obedient and turn to prayer and prostration such that an individual lowers his head to the ground.[241]

The Prophet ﷺ mentioned on another occasion, 'A true believer does not taunt, curse, involve himself in indecency or abuse others'.[242]

The Prophet ﷺ beautifully informed us, 'There is not indecency in anything except that the indecency defaces it and there is not modesty in anything except that it adorns it'.[243]

This noble character and abstention from any indecent talk extended to individuals of other religions as well, many of whom were constantly abusing the Prophet verbally and sometimes even physically. Once a group of Jews came to visit the Prophet ﷺ and greeted him by saying *As-Saam 'Alaykum* (which translates as 'death be upon you' instead of the proper greeting of *As-Salaam 'Alaykum* - may peace be

---

[240] Sahih al-Bukhari, Hadeeth number 6031.

[241] See: the following (and many other) commentaries for these and other explanations.
- Fath al-bari by Ibn Hajar, vol 1 page 92.
- Commentary of Ibn Battal for Sahih al-Bukhari, vol 9 page 242.
- 'Umdah al-qari by al-'Ayni, vol 32 page 214.
- Al-Kashif commentary of Mishkaat by at-Tibi, vol 12 page 3704.
- Tufah al-Abraar by Qadi Baydhawi, vol 3 page 471.

[242] Sunan at-Tirmidhi, vol 3 page 231, Hadeeth number 2092.

[243] Sunan at-Tirmidhi, vol 3 page 230, Hadeeth number 2089.

upon you), the wife of the Prophet ﷺ was understandably annoyed and began cursing them in return by saying, 'May the curse and anger of Allah befall you!' Immediately, the Prophet ﷺ told his wife to calm down and advised her to remain temperate and disciplined, to avoid harshness and coarseness.[244] The Prophet ﷺ simply replied to the group of Jews with, 'And upon you too (i.e. whatever you pray for me, I pray the very same for you)'.[245] He ﷺ never added any words of indecency from his own side.

Many individuals treat their employees, servants, women folk, etc. with indecency, oppression and abuse, our beloved mother, 'Aisha RA reports that she never witnessed the Prophet ﷺ ever hit any of his servants, wives or anybody (or even anything) else for that matter, the only exception was in the battle field.[246]

Furthermore, the great servant and student of the Prophet ﷺ, Anas ibn Malik رضي الله عنه mentions that I served the Prophet ﷺ for a period of 10 years, never once did he rebuke me in a defamatory manner.[247]

Sharaf ad-Din at-Teebi RA and a number of other scholars explain that indecency, shameless talk and immoral actions disgrace and deface an individual, whereas modesty always elevates an individual. They also mention that if indecency were to afflict even a non-human, it would disgrace it. Likewise, if modesty was imbued and diffused into any non-human, it would beautify it, then why would it not disgrace or beautify the human?[248]

Badr ad-Din ibn Jamaa'ah warns in the commentary of this narration, 'Unfortunately, many scholars and jurists of our era have been afflicted with indecency, this includes acts such as jealousy, pride, a yearning for fame and lacking of modesty'.

Zayn ad-Din al-Munaawi RA, a scholar who was born almost three centuries later adds, 'If only he (i.e. Badr ad-Din ibn Jamaa'ah RA) was to see the scholars of our time (where these unfortunate traits have further increased)'.[249]

May Almighty Allah protect us all, protect our scholars and keep us away from the net of the devil by becoming involved in jealousy, indecent talk, pride, lack of sincerity, a yearning for fame and lack of modesty; for indeed, the Prophet ﷺ is our best and most perfect role model whom we should always aspire to follow.

---

[244] Sahih al-Bukhari, hadeeth number 6030.
[245] Sahih al-Bukhari, hadeeth number 6024.
[246] Musnad of Imam Ahmad, hadeeth number 25923.
[247] Sunan at-Tirmidhi, vol 3 page 246, Hadeeth number 2134.
[248] Al-Kashif by at-Tibi, vol 10 page 3129.
[249] Faydh al-Qadeer by al-Munawi, vol 5 page 589.

لَمْ يَكُنِ النَّبِيُّ صَخَّابًا فِيْ الْأَسْوَاقِ

The Prophet ﷺ was not rowdy and unrestrained in the markets (public places)

(Sunan at-Tirmidhi)

When the mother of the believers was asked regarding the character of the Prophet ﷺ, she replied,

'The Prophet ﷺ was not indecent in his dealings, nor would he engage in any form of indecency, he was not rowdy and unrestrained in the markets and neither did he ever seek revenge for an evil that was personally committed towards him, rather he would pardon and forgive'.[250]

The reason for the specific mention of the Prophet ﷺ being civilised in the market is because it is known to be a place wherein shouting, argumentation and vulgarity is understood to be common. However, the Prophet ﷺ was a man of dignity and nobility in all scenarios, he would not stoop to screaming and shouting for bartering and bargaining or to acquire some worldly matter, the few instances in which the Prophet ﷺ did raise his voice were religiously motivated.[251]

The Prophet ﷺ once supplicated, 'May Allah shower His mercy upon the individual who adopts a gentle attitude whilst buying, selling and even when demanding the repayment of debts'.[252]

Abu al-Hasan ibn Battal RA comments, 'This prophetic narration encourages one to be gentle in his dealings with others and to adopt the best of character avoiding unnecessary disputes in transactions'. He adds, 'This will result in immense blessings in one's transactions as the Prophet ﷺ only directs humanity towards those deeds which benefit his followers in both worlds; the benefit in the hereafter is acquired via the (above) supplication of mercy made by the Prophet ﷺ, for indeed, whoever follows the advice of the Prophet ﷺ will be blessed with his supplication'.[253]

---

[250] Sunan at-Tirmidhi, vol 3 page 246, Hadeeth number 2135.

[251] See:

- Jam' al-Wasail by Mulla 'Ali al-Qari,
- Daleel al-Faliheen by ibn 'Allan, vol 4 page 382.

[252] Sahih al-Bukhari, hadeeth number 2076.

[253] Sharh ibn Battal, vol 6 page 211.

Fraud and deception is unfortunately extremely common amongst many merchants and business individuals, the Prophet ﷺ warned against such immoral behaviour with an extremely stern warning, he ﷺ mentioned, 'Allah will not talk to three people nor look at them (with mercy), neither will He purify them and for them is a severe punishment'. The Messenger of Allah ﷺ repeated this sentence three times after which Abu Dharr ﷺ enquired from the Prophet ﷺ, 'These people are certainly in failure and destruction in the Hereafter! Who are these people, Oh Messenger of Allah?' Upon this the Prophet ﷺ responded, 'They are; he who drags his lower garment (on the ground), the one who constantly recalls his favours upon others and the one who sells goods by making false oaths'.[254]

The Prophet ﷺ also informed us of an incident from the previous nations, 'An individual from the earlier generations passed away, he was then asked (by the angels) if he has any good deeds to his name. The individual replied in the negative, however, the angels probed him to ponder deeply. After much thought, the man replied, 'I am not aware of any good deed worthy of mention, except that I was a merchant who would strike deals with the people, I always made it a habit to extend the payment deadline for wealthy individuals (if they required more time) and I would forgive those that bought something from me and were struggling to pay for it'. The Prophet ﷺ then mentioned, 'Almighty Allah will mention I am more worthy of forgiving others and so Allah will then forgive him and enter him into paradise'.[255]

[254] Sahih Muslim, hadeeth number 306.
[255] Sahih al-Bukhari, hadeeth number 3451.

لَمْ يَكُنِ النَّبِيُّ يَجْزِي بِالسَّيِّئَةِ السَّيِّئَةَ وَلَكِنْ يَعْفُو وَيَصْفَحُ

The Prophet ﷺ would never avenge an evil with another evil, rather, he would forgive and forget

(Sahih al-Bukhari)

Forgiveness was an intrinsic quality resonant in the life of the Prophet ﷺ, the books which present the Prophetic biographical accounts have captured an incident regarding the Prophet ﷺ prior to the occurrence of the battle of Badr which demonstrates this quality.

The Prophet ﷺ was once riding a donkey which had a soft velvet cloth upon it, Usaamah ibn Zayd رضي الله عنه was the companion rider of the Prophet ﷺ in this journey wherein they intended to visit Sa'd ibn 'Ubaadah رضي الله عنه who was sick, he was from the locality of Banu al-Haarith al-Kazraj.

The Prophet ﷺ passed by a gathering in which a number of Muslims and non-Muslims were seated together, one of those individuals was 'Abdullah ibn Ubayy ibn Salul who was a non-Muslim (and held extreme hatred for the Prophet ﷺ), as the Prophet ﷺ was passing by, the dust caused by the animal affected the gathering, 'Abdullah ibn Ubayy covered his face with a cloth and (angrily) snapped at the Prophet ﷺ, 'Do not cover us in dust!' The Prophet ﷺ stopped, dismounted and warmly greeted them, he then went on to invite them towards Islam, he also read a portion of the Holy Qur'an to them.

'Abdullah ibn Ubayy was immediately annoyed with this recitation and preaching and so he quickly uttered, 'Oh man (i.e. Muhammad), nothing can be better than what you speak if it be the truth (however, I don't believe it to be the truth, hence your speech is not good)'. He then added, 'Do not disturb our gatherings with your speech, if somebody is interested in your talk, they will come to you'.

A number of Muslims in the gathering became extremely upset at how the Prophet ﷺ was spoken to and so they commented, 'Oh Prophet of Allah, visit us (more) in our gatherings, we love what you have to preach and say'. Unfortunately, the two groups began to quarrel which would very soon ensue into a fight. Immediately, the Prophet ﷺ demonstrated his wisdom at this delicate time by calming the people (and advising the Muslims not to take revenge).

The Prophet ﷺ then continued on his travel to visit the sick Sa'd ؓ, upon reaching Sa'd ؓ he ﷺ informed him of the incident that had occurred, Sa'd ؓ informed the Prophet ﷺ, 'The people of his town (i.e. Madinah) were ready to crown him (i.e. 'Abdullah ibn Ubayy) as the chief, however, when Allah sent you with the truth and the people chose to follow you instead of him, it tremendously irritated him and made him behave in an aggressive and hostile manner with you, the Prophet ﷺ immediately forgave him.[256]

The example of Prophet ﷺ and his forgiving attitude is also echoed by a number of great scholars and leaders from history; Mu'awiyah RA imparted a priceless piece of advice, he said, 'Until you gain a position of authority, hold firmly onto forbearance; once you are in a position of authority, hold firmly onto forgiveness'.[257]

The Umayyad caliph, Hisham ibn 'Abd al-Malik RA asked a pious individual why Dhul Qarnayn RA had been given the kingdom, power and authority he was given, the reply was that he had been blessed with four discerning characteristics; [1] When he had authority (over others) he would speedily forgive, [2] when he made a covenant with anyone, he would fulfil it, [3] whenever he spoke to anybody, he was always truthful, [4] he would never delay the job of today for tomorrow.[258]

Imam Ahmad RA was asked whether he would forgive those individuals who had tortured him, he answered by reciting the verse of the Qur'an, 'Whoever pardons and reconciles, then his reward is due from Almighty Allah'.[259] He then commented on the verse and explained, 'When it will be called out on the day of reckoning for those individuals to stand who have any outstanding reward due to them from Almighty Allah, only those individuals will stand who have forgiven others'. Imam Ahmad RA said, 'I have pardoned even those who are now dead from amongst the individuals who beat me and tortured me'.[260]

---

[256] Sahih al-Bukhari, Hadeeth number 6207.
[257] Ihya 'Ulum ad-Din, vol 3 page 184.
[258] Ihya 'Ulum ad-Din, vol 3 page 184.
[259] Surah ash-Shuraa, chapter 42 verse 40.
[260] Al-Adab as-Shari'yyah by Ibn Muflih, vol 1 page 92.

الرَّاحِمُوْنَ يَرْحَمُهُمُ الرَّحْمَنُ اِرْحَمُوْا أَهْلَ الْأَرْضِ يَرْحَمْكُمْ مَنْ فِيْ السَّمَاءِ

The merciful are shown mercy by The All-Merciful; show mercy towards the dwellers of the earth, and The Being in the heavens will shower mercy upon you

(Sunan abu Dawood)

The Prophet ﷺ mentioned, 'Show mercy to others and mercy will be showered upon you (by Almighty Allah), forgive others and Almighty Allah will forgive you. Woe to the vessels that catch words (i.e. the ears), woe to those who persist and insistently continue in whatever (evil) they are involved in'.[261]

Hafidh ibn Rajab RA comments, 'The vessels that catch words is referring to the notion that the ears are similar to vessels with holes on both sides, the good counsel and advice enters one ear and leaves through the other, however, unfortunately, the advice is not pondered upon nor is it processed by the brain, rather, it very quickly escapes through the other ear'.[262]

The Prophet ﷺ warned against the persistence upon evil without repenting, because 'persistence in sin directly leads towards leaving Islam in its entirety'.[263]

The Prophet ﷺ showed mercy to all humans irrespective of their religion; once, the Prophet ﷺ was asked to invoke a curse upon the polytheists, the Prophet ﷺ calmly replied, 'I have not been sent (into this world from Almighty Allah) as an invoker of curses, rather I have been sent as mercy'.[264]

Ibn al-Malak ar-Rumi RA mentions, 'The mercy of the Prophet ﷺ is clear, however, the mercy of the Prophet ﷺ directed towards the disbelievers has also been indicated to in the verse of the Holy Qur'an, 'And Allah will not punish the disbelievers (with an epidemic punishment) whilst you (Oh Muhammad) are still amongst them'.[265] So, from the many mercies of the Prophet ﷺ, his presence itself is a cause due to which an epidemic (general) punishment is averted and not sent upon the rebellious individuals (of Makkah).

---

[261] Al-Adab al-Mufrad by Imam al-Bukhari, Hadeeth number 380.

[262] Ghareeb al-Hadeeth by Ibn Qutaybah, vol 1 page 337 and Fath al-Bari by Ibn Rajab, vol 1 page 181.

[263] Fath al-Bari by Ibn Rajab, vol 1 page 181.

[264] Sahih Muslim, Hadeeth number 6778.

[265] Surah al-Anfal, verse 33.

To attract the immense mercy of Almighty Allah, one should be merciful towards the people of the earth, however, it is also imperative to beseech Almighty Allah directly through supplication for His mercy.

'Umar ibn 'Abd al-Azeez RA would regularly supplicate, 'Oh Allah, if I am not worthy of attaining your mercy, there is no doubt that your (vast) mercy is capable of reaching me, for your mercy encompasses everything and I am also a thing!'[266] He would add, 'Oh Allah, the most Merciful, You created the human to worship Yourself, yet Your mercy showered them prior to their worshipping You, (so Your mercy is not necessarily in need of good deeds)'.

The saints of the past would testify to the mercy of Almighty Allah in almost everything, even in the creation of hell-fire! The great scholar, Sufyan ibn 'Uyaynah RA mentioned, 'Almighty Allah created the fire as a form of mercy for mankind, it is by means of this fire that Almighty Allah deters His servants from evil (which will result in severe punishment in hell) so that they may refrain'.[267]

May Almighty Allah make us from the recipients of His immense mercy and may He allow us to be merciful towards others; including those that may be under our limited and temporary responsibility and trust.

[266] Hilyah al-Awliya', vol 6 page 2101.

[267] At-Takweef min an-Nar by Ibn Rajab, vol 1 page 34.

Narration 31

مَنْ كَانَ يُؤْمِنُ بِاللَّهِ وَالْيَوْمِ الآخِرِ فَلَا يُؤْذِ جَارَهُ

Whoever believes in Allah and the Last Day, should not harm their neighbour

(Sahih al-Bukhari)

The rights of the neighbour have been greatly emphasised in Islam, Almighty Allah mentions, 'Worship Almighty Allah and associate nothing with Him, also do good to parents, relatives, orphans, the needy, the neighbour who is near and to the neighbour who is distant...'[268]

The Prophet ﷺ even regarded the good word and approval of the neighbour as the gauge to measure one's goodness, a man asked the Prophet ﷺ, 'How am I to know if I have done well or if I have done bad?' The Prophet ﷺ replied, 'If you hear of your neighbours saying that you have done well, then you have indeed done well, and if you hear of them saying that you have done bad, then you have indeed done bad'.[269]

Al-Ameer as-San'aani RA mentions, 'Neighbours have been used as a yardstick for one's success and failure due to the great value placed in neighbours, some scholars have gone to the extent to mention that if an individual is amicable and friendly towards their neighbours, then their sins may be forgiven, whereas, if they are unpleasant towards their neighbours then their good conduct with others will be of little benefit'.[270]

The second caliph, 'Umar رضي الله عنه mentioned, 'If an individual is praised by their neighbour, relative and companion, then never complain (doubt) regarding their piety (indeed the praising of those in close proximity to an individual reveals the true colours of their piety and virtue)'.[271]

The Prophet ﷺ advised us to share our food with our neighbours, he ﷺ mentioned, 'Whenever you prepare a broth (and soup), increase the water therein, thereafter consider the homes of your neighbours and send them some of the prepared broth with courtesy (and kindness)'.[272]

---

[268] Surah an-Nisa, chapter 4 verse 36.
[269] Sunan Ibn Majah, Hadeeth number 4223.
[270] At-Tanweer Sharh al-Jami' as-Sagheer by al-Ameer as-Sana'ni, vol 2 page 98.
[271] Sharh as-Sunnah by Imam Baghawi, vol 13 page 73.
[272] Saheeh Muslim, Hadeeth number 6856.

'Awn ad-Din ibn Hubayrah RA mentioned, 'Many a time, the neighbour can smell food being prepared and they will become aware of the dish being prepared'.[273] Hence, in order to avoid them becoming saddened - especially if they are poor and unable to prepare such a dish - one should invite them to partake in the food, Almighty Allah will shower blessings in your food and fill the hearts of the neighbours with joy.

Ibn 'Umar ﷺ mentioned, 'We used to live in an era when the people loved their Muslim brothers more than their own wealth, however, we are now living in an era where people love their own wealth more than their Muslim brothers'. He then added, 'I heard the Prophet ﷺ mention regarding the sheer number of individuals who will be brought forth on the day of judgment by their neighbours, and the neighbours will complain to Allah, "Oh Lord, this is the very individual who closed his door upon me and refused to show me his kindness (and due rights as a neighbour)"'.[274]

Imam al-Qurtubi RA mentions, 'The advices provided regarding the rights of the neighbour is thoroughly emphasised and it extends to the non-Muslim neighbour as well as the Muslim neighbour'.[275]

Imam al-Ghazzali RA mentions, 'The rights of the neighbour are not simply limited to being cautious so as not to harm them, rather, from their rights is to assist them in their moments of difficulty (and to carry their burden for them)'. He then adds, 'Even this is not sufficient, rather it is necessary to go a step further by being courteous to them by sending gifts, food etc.'[276]

---

[273] Al-Ifsah 'An M'ani as-Sihah, vol 2 page 195.
[274] Al-Adab al-Mufrad, Hadeeth number 111.
[275] Tafseer al-Qurtubi, vol 5 page 184.
[276] Ihya 'Ulum ad-Din, vol 2 page 56.

مَنْ كَانَ يُؤْمِنُ بِاللَّهِ وَالْيَوْمِ الآخِرِ فَلْيُكْرِمْ ضَيْفَهُ

Whoever believes in Allah and the Last Day, then they should honour their guest

(Sahih al-Bukhari)

The Prophet ﷺ mentioned, 'No day dawns upon the servants (of Allah) except that they are visited by two angels, one of them supplicates, 'Oh Allah, grant the individual who spends (for Your sake) a worthy reward (in this world and the Hereafter)', and the other angel supplicates, 'Oh Allah, bring destruction to the individual who withholds (his money from spending for Your sake)'.[277]

Imam Nawawi RA mentions in his commentary of this narration, 'The spending that is desired includes the money spent in the performance of virtuous deeds, spending towards the acquisition of good manners (and improving society), spending upon one's family and guests, and all other forms of charitable causes. On the other hand, the prayer of destruction is for those individuals who withhold money from these very same causes'.[278]

Hosting and honouring the guest is from the noble qualities of all the Prophets, Almighty Allah has praised the Prophet Ibrahim عليه السلام in the Holy Qur'an for his warm and cordial hospitality of his guests, Allah mentions, 'Has the story reached you of the honourable guests of Ibrahim? (It was) When the angels entered upon Ibrahim and they said "Peace be with you", Ibrahim replied, "Peace be upon you too", he then said, "(You are) unknown people (and not locals)". The Prophet Ibrahim then slipped away to his family (to arrange some food for the guests), he returned with a juicy calf (which was roasted) and he placed the food before them"'.[279]

Some commentators have mentioned that the Prophet Ibrahim عليه السلام never directly addressed the guests (angels) as 'unknown people', rather, he either said it to himself or to his family members, for, such a statement may embarrass the guests.[280]

---

[277] Sahih al-Bukhari, Hadeeth number 1442.
[278] Al-Minhaj by an-Nawawi, vol 3 page 450.
[279] Surah ad-Dhariyat, surah number 51, verse number 24-27.
[280] Al-Bahr al-Muheet by Abu Hayyan al-Andalusi, vol 9 page 555.

Hafidh ibn Katheer RA mentions, 'These verses (demonstrating the hospitality of the Prophet Ibrahim عليه السلام) comprise of the etiquettes of hosting a guest', a number of them are outlined below:

1. He brought the food in a manner wherein the guests were unaware of it being brought,
2. He brought the food as quickly as he possibly could,
3. He never made the guests feel uncomfortable by asking them if they wanted to eat, rather, he made the arrangements without even asking,
4. He brought the best of the food that he could arrange,
5. He placed the food directly in front of them, not burdening the guest of taking the food closer to them, the guests may feel ashamed of doing so.[281]

Hafidh ibn al-Qayyim RA[282] indicates to a number of additional lessons that can be derived from this incident of the Prophet Ibrahim عليه السلام and his hospitality, he mentions,

'The guests arrived without seeking prior permission (which is conventionally sought), the reason for this was because the hospitality of Prophet Ibrahim عليه السلام was well known to the public as his door was always open for guests without appointment, such was the generosity of Prophet Ibrahim'.

'The speed at which the Prophet Ibrahim عليه السلام brought the calf from his own family suggests that they had it prepared (or they were habitual in hosting guests at short notice), they never needed any support from neighbours or anyone else indicating to the ever-ready nature of Prophet Ibrahim عليه السلام in regard to hosting guests'.

'The Prophet Ibrahim عليه السلام brought the food with his own hands, he never ordered a worker or a servant to bring the food, this demonstrates the degree of respect and esteem he held of his guests'.

The Prophet ﷺ also advised us in regard to the minimum period of time one should cater for their guest but also that the guest should be cautious so as not to burden the host beyond their individual and personal capability. The Prophet ﷺ mentioned, 'The (recommended) period of hosting a guest is three days (it is from the Islamic rights and manners that an individual host the guest for a period of at least three days), and it is bonus act of kindness to host for an additional day (so in total, to

[281] Tafseer Ibn Katheer, vol 7 page 421.

[282] Jila' al-Afhaam by Ibn al-Qayyim, page 274. He mentions 15 etiquettes for hosting guests from the incident of Prophet Ibrahim AS and mentions these are comprehensive guidelines for hosting guests.

host the guest for a period of four days), it is not permissible for a Muslim to extend their stay so much that it makes him (the host) sinful (as it is possible that he takes a lax attitude in fulfilling the rights of the guest)'. The companions enquired, 'Oh Messenger of Allah, how would a guest make the host sinful?' Allah's Messenger ﷺ replied, 'He stays with the host for such a lengthy period that nothing is left with the host to give to the guest'.[283]

The Prophet ﷺ practically taught all guests to pray and supplicate for the host, he ﷺ was once a guest at the house of a companion and he gave the Prophet ﷺ (and others) food, drink and dates, when the Prophet ﷺ was leaving, he supplicated for the family, 'Oh Allah, bless them in what you have provided them, forgive them and have mercy upon them'.[284]

[283] Sahih Muslim, Hadeeth number 4611.
[284] Sunan Abu Dawood, Hadeeth number 3729.

مَنْ كَانَ يُؤْمِنُ بِاللهِ وَالْيَوْمِ الآخِرِ فَلْيَقُلْ خَيْرًا أَوْ لِيَصْمُتْ

Whoever believes in Allah and the Last Day, should either speak good or remain silent

(Sahih al-Bukhari)

'Abdullah ibn Abi Awfa ﵁ mentioned, 'The Prophet ﷺ would remember Almighty Allah abundantly, he would seldom engage in idle talk, he would lengthen the prayer and shorten the sermon and the Prophet ﷺ would not shy away from walking with a widow or a needy individual to attend to their needs'.[285]

Imam as-Suyuti RA has mentioned, 'Seldomly engaging in idle talk actually refers to the absolute absence of idle talk'.[286]

Imam as-Sindhi RA mentions, 'Seldomly engaging in idle talk refers to how the Prophetic speech was frequently filled with comprehensive and meaningful nuances, from his speech, very little of it lacked this quality'.[287]

The great Companion, ibn 'Abbas ﵁ would hold his tongue and chastise himself, 'Only speak that which is upright and you will benefit, remain silent from that which is harmful and you will be protected'. A person once asked ibn 'Abbas ﵁ regarding his actions and ibn 'Abbas ﵁ replied, 'It has reached me (from the Prophet ﷺ) that on the day of reckoning, an individual will be most angry with his tongue'.[288]

Many a time, we become involved in futile arguments and debates, the Prophet ﷺ has always emphasised the adoption of the best manners and to leave argumentation even when an individual is correct. He ﷺ mentioned, 'I guarantee a house on the outskirts of Paradise for an individual who avoids quarrelling even if he is right, I guarantee a house in the centre of Paradise for the individual who avoids lying even if it be in jest, and I guarantee a house in the uppermost part of Paradise for the individual who beautifies themselves with impeccable character'.[289]

Abu al-Faraj ibn al-Jawzi RA mentions, 'The Prophet 'Isa عليه السلام was asked regarding an action that can qualify an individual for entry into Paradise, he replied, "Always

---

[285] Sunan an-Nasai', Hadeeth number 1414.
[286] Footnotes of Imam as-Suyuti on Sunan an-Nasai', vol 2 page 461.
[287] Footnotes of Imam As-Sindi on Sunan an-Nasai', vol 2 page 461.
[288] Az-Zuhd by Imam Ahmad, Narration number 1037. Also see: Al-Mu'jam al-Kabeer by Imam at-Tabrani, narration number 10294.
[289] Sunan Abu Dawood, Hadeeth number 4802.

remain silent", the people objected due to the necessity of speech (as it is impossible to remain entirely silent), 'Isa عليه السلام then responded, "Only ever speak the good (restrain your tongue from speaking or indulging in any evil talk)"'.[290] The pious predecessors recognised the importance of adopting silence, yet they also appreciated the mammoth nature of this task for the general public.

Muhammad ibn Wasi' RA mentioned to Malik ibn Dinar RA, 'Indeed controlling (and safeguarding) one's tongue is more difficult a task for the people than safeguarding their own wealth'.[291]

It is mentioned regarding Ar-Rabi ibn Khuthaym RA that he abandoned worldly-talk for twenty years, rather he would busy himself with studies; his pen and paper.[292]

Ar-Rabi ibn Khuthaym RA would mention, 'There is little benefit in talk except in nine cases, [1] Expressing the oneness of Almighty Allah *(tahleel),* [2] Extolling and enthusiastically praising the greatness of Almighty Allah *(takbeer),* [3] Exalting the purity of Almighty Allah *(tasbeeh),* [4] Praising Almighty Allah *(tahmeed),* [5] Enquiring regarding good matters (seeking knowledge), [6] Seeking protection from evil, [7] Enjoining the good, [8] Forbidding the evil, [9] Reading the Holy Qur'an'.[293]

---

[290] Bahr ad-Dumu' by Abu al-Faraj ibn al-Jawzi, page 100.
[291] Ihya 'Ulum ad-Din, vol 3 page 111.
[292] Ihya 'Ulum ad-Din, vol 3 page 111.
[293] As-Samt by Ibn Abu Dunya, page 84.

مَنْ يُحْرَمِ الرِّفْقَ يُحْرَمِ الْخَيْرَ

Whoever is deprived of gentleness is deprived of goodness

(Sahih Muslim)

Almighty Allah sent the Prophet Musa عليه السلام and the Prophet Harun عليه السلام to converse with the Pharaoh (leader) who had oppressed the Israelite nation such that he even murdered an innumerable amount of their children. Almighty Allah advised the Prophet Musa عليه السلام thus; '(Oh Musa) You and your brother go (to Pharaoh) with my miraculous signs, and do not become negligent in My remembrance, the both of you go to Pharaoh for he has transgressed, speak to him compassionately, perhaps he will accept the advice or maybe even fear Allah (and retract from his transgressions and oppression)'.[294]

An individual read these verses in the presence of the great saint, Yahya ibn Mu'aadh ar-Razi RA, Yahya RA began to cry profusely and exclaimed, 'Oh Allah, how compassionate your approach is with an individual who claims himself to be God (i.e. Pharaoh), what level of compassion will you show the individual who accepts You, Oh Allah, as God?!'[295]

The great commentator of the Qur'an, Imam al-Aalusi RA mentions in the commentary of this verse, 'This verse is proof that an individual should speak with courtesy even when advising an oppressor, for, maybe the oppressor will take heed from the advice (due to the polite gentle demeanour)'.[296]

Imam al-Qurtubi RA mentions, 'Every individual should endeavour to speak politely with others and meet them with a smiling face irrespective of whether they are religious or not... because Almighty Allah ordered the Prophet Musa عليه السلام and the Prophet Harun عليه السلام to speak politely with Pharaoh and there is no speaker (today) who holds more virtue than the Prophet Musa عليه السلام and the Prophet Harun عليه السلام, nor is any individual who is being spoken too worse than the Pharaoh; despite that, Almighty Allah ordered both of them to speak politely with Pharaoh'.[297]

---

[294] Surah Taha, chapter 20 verse 42-44.
[295] Tafseer al-Khazin, vol 3 page 205.
[296] Ruh al-Ma'ni by Al-Alusi, vol 8 page 508.
[297] Tafseer al-Qurtubi, vol 2 page 16.

Even the greatest of all teachers, the Prophet ﷺ was instructed to be lenient with his visitors and companions. Almighty Allah mentions, 'It is only through the mercy of Almighty Allah that you (Oh Muhammad) were lenient with them (your companions), for, if you had been rude and harsh-hearted, they would have abandoned you'.[298]

Imam ar-Razi RA mentions that when one converses with others; whether the talk is religious or worldly, if the discussion can be concluded cordially and amicably, then it would be nonsensical to resort to any other manner, he then goes on to provide the incidents of the Prophets Musa عليه السلام and Harun عليه السلام and also the aforementioned verse relative to the Prophet ﷺ as proof for this claim.[299]

The Prophet ﷺ emphasised this idea with his statement, 'Whoever has been given a share of compassion, indeed they have been given a share of goodness, and whoever has been prevented from a share of compassion, then they have truly been prevented from their share of goodness'.[300]

A Bedouin once urinated in the mosque, some individuals jumped up (to reprimand him), however, the Prophet ﷺ instructed, 'Do not interrupt him as he relieves the call of nature', it was then that the Prophet ﷺ asked for a bucket of water and poured it over the urine.[301]

Scholars have reiterated this incident of the Prophet ﷺ as the perfect example of compassion, especially with an unlearned and innocent person, the Bedouin was unaware of the protocols of the mosque, the sanctity of the mosque, and so the Prophet ﷺ permitted him to finish urinating; however, once he had finished urinating and the area was cleaned, the Prophet ﷺ called him forth and respectfully educated him regarding the inappropriate nature of urinating in the mosque.[302]

'Aisha RA narrated from her husband (the Prophet ﷺ), 'When Almighty Allah intends to bring goodness into a household, he blesses them with gentleness'.[303]

Abu ad-Darda' ﷺ mentioned, 'A sign of intellect within an individual is his gentleness with his family'.[304]

---

[298] Surah 'Ali 'Imran, surah 3 verse 159.

[299] Mafateeh al-gayb, vol 3 page 589.

[300] Sunan at-Tirmidhi, vol 3 page 245, Hadeeth number 2132.

[301] Saheeh al-Bukhari, Hadeeth number 6025.

[302] Fath al-Mun'im by Musa Saheen, vol 2 page 244.

[303] Musnad Imam Ahmad, Hadeeth number 24427.

[304] Az-Zuhd by Hannad ibn al-Sirry, narration number 1437.

مِنْ حُسْنِ إِسْلَامِ الْمَرْءِ تَرْكُهُ مَا لَا يَعْنِيهِ

From the perfection of an individual's faith is to forsake that which does not concern them

(Sunan at-Tirmidhi)

The Prophet ﷺ mentioned, 'From the perfection of an individual's faith is to forsake that which does not concern him'.[305] Hafidh ibn al-Qayyim RA mentions, 'This comprises the abandonment of idle talk, the reading and viewing of futile content and material, listening to the unnecessary and pointless, thinking of that which is insignificant and any other worthless esoteric (inner) or exoteric (outer) action; indeed this advice of the Prophet ﷺ is the most comprehensive in the chapter of piety'.[306]

Imam ibn al-'Arabi RA mentions, 'The motive for leaving that which is futile and it being regarded as the perfection of an individual's faith is because one does not have the time in life to even fulfil those deeds which are of the highest priority and so why would anybody waste (precious) time in that which is of no avail to them?'[307]

Imam Abu Dawood RA mentioned, 'The four core prophetic narrations are as follows: [1] All actions are (rewarded) in accordance to the intentions, [2] The permitted is evident, the prohibited is evident, between the two lies the doubted, whoever refrains from the doubted has protected their religion and their honour, [3] From the perfection of an individual's faith is to forsake that which does not concern them, [4] Abstain from the materialistic (and that which is worldly) and Allah will love you, abstain from (yearning for) that which the people have and the people will love you'.[308]

In the scrolls of Prophet Ibrahim عليه السلام, it is mentioned, 'Whosoever appreciates their speech as being from amongst the deeds (which one will be questioned regarding), then they would limit their speech to that which is beneficial (i.e. they would abandon all futile talk)'.[309]

---

[305] Sunan at-Tirmidhi, vol 3 page 409, Hadeeth number 2472.
[306] Madarij as-Salikeen, vol 2 page 21.
[307] Sharh az-Zurqani 'Ala Muwatta, vol 4 page 317.
[308] At-Tamheed by Ibn Abd al-Barr, vol 9 page 201. Imam an-Nawawi has recorded from Imam Ibn as-Salah that the views of different scholars regarding the core narrations of religion can be gather as 26 narrations; Imam an-Nawawi has mentioned the 26 in his Bustan al-'Arifeen, page 4.
[309] Al-Idhtidhkaar by Ibn Abd al-Barr, vol 9 page 255.

Hind ibn Abu Haalah RA mentions regarding the speech of the Prophet ﷺ, 'The Prophet ﷺ was always concerned (about the hereafter and the interrogation one will be subject to for every deed and every word), he ﷺ was always in deep thought and contemplation, he would rest very little (as his concern was of the hereafter), he would remain silent for lengthy periods, he would only speak if the need to speak presented itself, he would begin and end his speech with the name of Almighty Allah'.[310]

Jamal ad-Din al-Qasmi RA mentions, 'The most valuable wealth of an individual is their time, and every minute spent in futile deeds and speech is a minute lost in capturing the rewards of the hereafter, indeed, this individual has lost their most valuable wealth'. He advises as to how one can cure the wastage of their time too, he comments, 'An individual should ponder and introspect upon every breath (and every moment that passes) as being their most valuable wealth (and they have the option to use it in their favour or they can waste it). This individual should consider their tongue as a snare and trap by which they can capture the eternal goodness, therefore, wasting the energy of the tongue (in futility) is a great loss!'[311]

The great scholar, Ibrahim an-Nakha'i RA mentioned, 'Indeed, an excess in speech and an excess in wealth has destroyed the people'.[312]

The very same scholar, Ibrahim an-Nakha'i RA was asked regarding the one who totally abandons earning money and entirely focusses on acts of devotions and another who performs the necessary prayers, however, he commits time to earning a living too, who is the better of the two? Ibrahim an-Nakha'i RA replied, 'The honest businessman (who devoted a portion of his time to earn a pure livelihood)'.[313]

This demonstrates that Islam is a religion of balance and equilibrium, the Prophet ﷺ is not advising us to abandon the world and anything associated with it, rather it is the excessive speech and money that we have been advised to distance ourselves from. Indeed, the earning of wealth in moderation with the intention of fulfilling one's needs, the needs of one's parents, partner, children, for giving in charity to the poor etc. is not branded as excessive wealth, rather, if one has the correct intention for their earnings, then that very earning becomes a form of worship.

---

[310] As-Shamail al-Muhammadiyyah by Imam at-Tirmidhi, Hadeeth number 226.
[311] Maw'idhah al-Mumineen by Jamal ad-Din al-Qasmi, page 187.
[312] Al-Adab as-Shar'iyyah by Ibn Muflih, vol 3 page 431.
[313] Al-Adab as-Shar'iyyah by Ibn Muflih, vol 3 page 430.

أَدِّ الْأَمَانَةَ إِلَى مَنِ ائْتَمَنَكَ وَلَا تَخُنْ مَنْ خَانَكَ

Fulfil the trust to the one who entrusts you, and do not betray the one who betrays you

(Sunan Abu Dawood)

Safeguarding and fulfilling the trust that is entrusted to an individual and distancing oneself from betrayal and treachery are from the essential teachings of Islam, irrelevant of whether another individual betrays us, a believer should always aspire to lead by example and fulfil (to the best of their ability) any trusts they have been assigned with, whether this trust be in the form of money, valuables or even in the form of speech and a secret matter.

The Prophet ﷺ mentioned, 'When an individual discusses something (in secrecy) and then turns away, that discussion becomes a trust between the two individuals'.[314]

Mudhir ad-Din az-Zaydani RA explains the narration, 'Once the two individuals separate, the talk that took place within the gathering becomes a trust which cannot be spread to others'.[315]

Imam at-Teebi RA also explains the narration, 'If somebody informs you of something whilst glancing to the left and right, then treat this information as a secret, for, he does not want anyone else to hear it and for you to spread this information to anybody else is a betrayal of the trust'.[316]

Another trust that is stressed in the Prophetic traditions is the secrets and the private moments shared between partners. The Prophet ﷺ mentioned, 'The greatest breach of trust (to be judged) on the day of judgment in the sight of Almighty Allah is of a man who goes to his wife (for intimacy) and she reciprocates and returns the love, however, he then spreads her secrets'.[317]

The Prophet ﷺ prophesised the unfortunate times to come when trusts will be abandoned. He ﷺ mentioned, 'Before the end of time, the trustworthy will be labelled as the dishonest and the dishonest will be labelled as the trustworthy'.[318]

---

[314] Sunan Abu Dawood, Hadeeth number 4868.
[315] Al-Mafatih, vol 5 page 247.
[316] Al-Kashf by Sharaf ad-Din at-Teebi, vol 10 page 3225.
[317] Saheeh Muslim, Hadeeth number 3616.
[318] Musnad Imam Ahmad, Hadeeth number 6872.

It was once that the Prophet ﷺ was asked when the world would end, he ﷺ responded with, 'When honesty is lost, then wait for the Last Hour'. He ﷺ was then asked, 'How will honesty be lost, Oh Messenger of Allah?' He ﷺ replied, 'When authority is offered to those who are not worthy (due to a lack of ability), then wait for the Last Hour'.[319]

Shihab ad-Din al-Qastallani RA mentions that this trust being handed to the wrong people even includes a judge or an individual providing Islamic verdicts.[320] This explanation is supported by various Prophetic teachings wherein he ﷺ mentions, 'Allah does not remove knowledge by extracting it from (the hearts of) the people; however, He removes it by causing the death of religious scholars such that no religious scholar will remain, the people shall then make the uneducated (ignorant) people their leaders, who, upon consultation shall give their religious verdicts (*fatwa*) without (having sufficient) knowledge. Hence, they will go astray and lead the people astray'.[321]

In an extremely alarming narration, the Prophet ﷺ warned of a time that will come when 'people will conduct mutual transactions, however, they will not fulfil the trusts',[322] he ﷺ then indicated that trustworthiness will be so scarce that people will be able to count the remaining trustworthy individuals left within society on their fingers.

Imam Bukhari RA reiterates this point by mentioning that the greatest priority for the dying individual is to 'fulfil that which they have been entrusted with, rather than making optional wills'.[323]

The fourth caliph, 'Ali رضي الله عنه beautifully advises in Arabic poetry, 'Fulfil your trusts and refrain from dishonesty, be just (in your dealings) and do not oppress, (as a result of which) your earning will be pleasant for you'.[324]

---

[319] Sahih al-Bukhari, Hadeeth number 6496.
[320] Irshad as-Sari by al-Qastallani, vol 1 page 155.
[321] Sahih al-Bukhari, Hadeeth number 102.
[322] Sahih al-Bukhari, Hadeeth number 7086.
[323] Sahih al-Bukhari, prior to Hadeeth number 2750.
[324] Diwan 'Ali ibn Abu Talib, page 58.

لَا تَجْلِسْ بَيْنَ رَجُلَيْنِ إِلَّا بِإِذْنِهِمَا

Do not sit between two except with their permission

(Sunan Abu Dawood)

Islam is a complete way of life which teaches the etiquette for all aspects of life. Seeking permission to enter upon a private gathering or place is also from the upright etiquette taught by Islam.

Almighty Allah mentions, 'Oh you who believe, do not enter any house other than your own unless you seek permission beforehand and then greet the inmates therein, that is virtuous for you so that you may be attentive and polite. If you do not find anyone therein, do not enter until permission is given to you'.[325]

Hafidh ibn Katheer RA mentioned, 'These verses indicate to the religious guidelines relative to seeking permission prior to entry which Almighty Allah has instructed his servants with'.[326] Scholars have made mention of a number of etiquettes that should be taken into consideration at the time of seeking permission, a number of them are below:

Firstly, an individual should seek permission no more than three times, if they are granted permission then they may enter, otherwise they should turn away. The Companion, Abu Musa al-Ash'ari ﵁ sought permission to enter upon 'Umar ﵁ and he sought permission thrice, however, Umar ﵁ did not respond, hence, Abu Musa ﵁ turned away. 'Umar ﵁ (who had heard his seeking permission) enquired from the people around him, 'Did you not hear the voice of Abu Musa ﵁ (seeking permission)? Call him and grant him permission'. When Abu Musa ﵁ returned, he was quizzed by 'Umar ﵁ as to why he went away after seeking permission thrice, he replied, 'This is what we have been taught (by the Prophet ﷺ)'.[327] Imam al-Qurtubi RA makes an addition at this juncture and point by commenting that if the seeker of permission knows for a fact that the individual they are seeking permission from never heard them, then they may go beyond the three times of seeking permission.[328]

---

[325] Surah an-Nur, surah 24 verse 27-28.
[326] Tafseer Ibn Katheer, vol 6 page 36.
[327] Saheeh Muslim, Hadeeth number 5757.
[328] Tafsir al-Qurtubi, vol 12 page 214.

Secondly, one should not stand directly in front of the door, rather they should stand to the right or the left of the door, 'Abdullah ibn Busr ؓ mentions that when the Prophet ﷺ went to anybody's house, he did not stand directly in front of the door, rather he stood to the right or the left of the door.[329] A man peeped through a hole in the residence of the Prophet ﷺ whilst the Prophet ﷺ had an iron comb in his hand with which he was combing his head, the Prophet ﷺ exclaimed, 'Had I known that you were looking (through the hole), I would have poked your eye with the comb, verily, the command of taking permission to enter another's home (or even their room) has been ordained to prevent this very peeping and seeing others (in their privacy) unlawfully'.[330]

Another etiquette of seeking permission is to respond appropriately when asked any questions, for example, if an individual is quizzed with the words, 'Who is it?' Then one should respond with such a name that will not leave any ambiguity in the mind of the individual granting permission, do not suffice with "It's me!" because anyone can be "me"! Jabir ؓ narrated, 'I came to the Prophet ﷺ in order to consult with him in regard to my father's debt, when I knocked on the door, he ﷺ asked, 'Who is it?' I replied, 'Me', he ﷺ replied, 'Me, me!' He repeated it as though he disliked it (and wished to show it)'.

An additional etiquette of seeking permission is to preface with the words of peace and salutations *(As salaamu 'alaykum wa rahmatullahi wa barakaatuh)* and to seek permission with wording that is appropriate. A man from the Banu 'Amir (tribe) informed us that he once asked the Prophet ﷺ for permission (to enter the house) with the words, 'I'm coming in, okay?'[331] The Prophet ﷺ replied to his servant, 'Go out to this individual and educate him of the correct method to seek permission for entering the house, advise him to say, "Peace be upon you (i.e *salaam)*, may I enter?"' The man took the advice and asked, 'Peace be upon you! May I enter?' The Prophet ﷺ permitted him entry and the man entered.[332]

A further religious etiquette is to knock gently (but loud enough for those inside to hear), the Companion, Anas ibn Malik ؓ mentioned, 'The Companions would knock on the doors of the Prophet ﷺ with their fingertips'.[333]

Finally, religious etiquette also necessitates an individual to not sit in the private gathering of two individuals, except with their permission.[334]

---

[329] Sunan Abu Dawood, Hadeeth number 5188.

[330] Sahih al-Bukhari, Hadeeth number 6241.

[331] The Arabic phrase used was not the most appropriate phrase for seeking permission

[332] Sunan Abu Dawood, Hadeeth number 5177.

[333] Al-Adab al-Mufrad, Hadeeth number 1080.

[334] Sunan Abu Dawood, Hadeeth number 4844. See, Daleel al-Faliheen by Ibn 'Allan, vol 6 page 118.

كُلُوْا مِنَ الطَّيِّبَاتِ

Eat from the pure

(Sahih Muslim)

Eating from the pure and the permissible (*halal*) is an extremely vital etiquette of Islam, the Prophet ﷺ has warned that if an individual is not cautious in regard to that which they consume (whether it is permitted or not), then there is a chance that their supplications to Almighty Allah will not be answered.

He ﷺ set the scene of a man who is travelling, his hair is dishevelled and covered with dust due to the longevity of his journey, he raises his hands towards the sky (and supplicates thus), 'O Lord, O Lord!' Whereas his food is unlawful, his drink is unlawful, his clothes are unlawful and his nourishment is unlawful, for, how then can his supplication be accepted?[335]

Shihab ad-Din at-Turibishti RA mentions, 'The Prophet ﷺ is actually referring to the annual pilgrimage (Hajj) in this narration (when speaking of the journey) wherein an individual undergoes much difficulty and inconvenience (in such a sacred travel coupled with difficulties, one would rightfully hope his supplications to be accepted) and he then begins to supplicate to Almighty Allah, however, unfortunately, his supplications are not accepted as he conducts impermissible dealings'.[336]

Mulla 'Ali al-Qari RA comments, 'This hadeeth indicates that consuming the lawful leads to an increase in pious deeds and actions by which a person gains proximity to Almighty Allah (whereas consuming the unlawful would result in a lack of pious deeds, rather, it can even lead an individual towards sin which takes a person further away from Almighty Allah and Paradise).[337]

The Prophetic advices make mention that one of the purest and most preferred forms of eating is that food which one has earned with their own hands, earning with one's own hands was also the practice of the Prophets peace be upon them.[338]

One should not suffice themselves with making 'easy' money if it is illegal or at the very least not the purest of income, rather, one should strive to make their money the purest they possibly can, and one of the best ways to achieve this is to physically

[335] Sahih Muslim, Hadeeth number 2393.
[336] Al-Muyassar by at-Turibishti, vol 2 page 655.
[337] Mirqaat al-Mafateeh, vol 5 page 1889.
[338] Saheeh al-Bukhari, Hadeeth number 2072.

earn a livelihood, it is without doubt that the wage an individual receives in exchange of hard work and toil is indeed the best of income. Scholars have mentioned that earning the minimum amount for one's individual survival and those dependant (family, etc.) is necessary, to earn beyond this is completely acceptable so long as it does not lead to any sins.[339]

The Prophet ﷺ warned that 'a time would come when none will care for how they gained their money; legally or illegally'.[340] Mufti Muhammad Taqi Usmani mentions, 'Unfortunately, it is becoming increasingly common in our era for people to no longer care regarding the lawful and unlawful'.[341]

In order to make the wealth pure, one should also make every effort to abstain from the doubtful, the Prophet ﷺ mentioned, 'The permitted is evident, the prohibited is evident, between the two lies the doubted, whoever refrains from the doubted has protected their religion and their honour, whereas, the individual who indulges themselves with the doubted is like a shepherd who grazes his animals near the private pastures of another, it is highly likely that the animals will stray into the private pastures'. Thereafter, the Prophet ﷺ mentioned, 'Oh people, beware! Every king has a private pasture, the private pasture of Almighty Allah on this earth are the deeds He has deemed unlawful, so keep at a lengthy distance from the unlawful, lest you stray into them'.[342]

Hafidh Ibn Hajar RA mentions, 'This narration indicates that the one who does not refrain from doubtful earnings should prepare himself for accusations (and other consequences)'.[343] He also mentions that 'this narration regarding the "doubtful" includes all aspects of life; financial dealings, marriage, food, etc'.[344]

---

[339] Mirqaat al-Mafateeh, vol 5 page 1889.
[340] Sahih al-Bukhari, Hadeeth number 2059.
[341] In'am al-Bari by Mufti Taqi al-Uthmani, vol 6 page 100.
[342] Saheeh al-Bukhari, Hadeeth number 52.
[343] Fath al-Bari, vol 1 page 127.
[344] Fath al-Bari, vol 4 page 291.

خَيْرُ الْأَصْحَابِ عِنْدَ اللَّهِ خَيْرُهُمْ لِصَاحِبِهِ

The best individual in the sight of Allah is the one who is best towards their companions

(Sunan at-Tirmidhi)

Treating one's colleagues, friends and associates in a good-natured manner is from amongst the rewarding acts in Islam. The vast majority of people, rightfully so, treat their acquaintances and companions pleasantly without even knowing that this action, if done with a noble intention, merits immense reward.

The Prophet ﷺ mentioned, 'The best individual in the sight of Almighty Allah is the one who is best towards their companions'.[345]

Mulla 'Ali al-Qari RA explains, 'The friend who will receive the most reward by Almighty Allah is the one who treats his acquaintances (this could include family members, friends, work colleagues etc.) amicably by interacting in an agreeable manner and granting favours, even if it be simple advice'.[346]

The Prophet ﷺ mentioned, 'The religion (of Islam) is to wish well and advise (with sincerity)', he ﷺ was asked for whom this well-wishing is for, the Prophet Muhammad ﷺ replied, 'Sincerity is shown to Allah (by following his commands), for His Book (by accepting it as the truth and following it's instructions), for His messengers (by accepting them as Prophets and emulating them), for the leaders of the Muslims (by obedience to them in those matters which don't violate the Islamic rulings and advising them in those matters they may err in) and for the general Muslims (by protecting their wealth and honour and removing all harm from them in the most appropriate manner)'.[347]

The Prophet ﷺ mentioned an essential etiquette in regard to companionship, he advises, 'When there are three of you sat together, then two of you should not talk secretly whilst excluding the third person, (do not do this) until you are joined by other people, because the two of you conversing secretly might upset the third'.[348]

This etiquette for acquaintances is to be observed in all scenarios, regardless of whether the individuals are travelling together, living together, studying together or

---

[345] Sunan at-Tirmidhi, vol 3 page 218, Hadeeth number 2057.

[346] Mirqaat al-Mafateeh, vol 8 page 3124.

[347] Sahih Muslim, Hadeeth number 205. Also see: Mirqaat al-Mafateeh, vol 7 page 3111.

[348] Sahih al-Bukhari, Hadeeth number 6290.

even working together. An example of this in the work place is if there are three individuals working on a single project and two from amongst them begin to talk privately (in the presence of the third) all the while excluding the third, then this should be avoided, for, this could cause grief and pain to the third person and he may feel that the two are talking privately regarding him or that they don't trust him with a secret. However, if there are more than three individuals, then two can talk privately as the third person is not alone, rather he has others around to talk with as well and he will not feel singled out.[349]

Another etiquette for acquaintances is to wish for one's companion that which one wishes for themselves. Many students and employees will be able to relate easily to scenarios wherein competition becomes unhealthy; a worker is trying to get another sacked or demoted unfairly in the hope that they can get promoted instead, or even worse, an individual acts out of jealousy with the only intent to stop the progress of another. This is totally against the etiquette of companionship, the Prophet ﷺ mentioned, 'None amongst you truly believes until they love for their brother that which they love for themselves'.[350]

Once the Prophet ﷺ mentioned, 'The inmates of Paradise are three: [1] The just ruler, who spends upon the people and is given the divine ability to do good, [2] The individual who shows mercy and kindness towards their close relatives and all Muslims, [3] The pious person (who stays away from the prohibited) and who refrains from begging despite having a (large) family'.

The Prophet ﷺ then mentioned that, 'The inmates of the Hellfire are five: [1] The weak who refuse to exert their willpower (to prevent themselves from committing sins) whilst pursuing everything with greed (and not avoiding the prohibited), yet, they do not search for a lawful partner for life and lawful wealth, [2] The dishonest person whose greed is commonly known, he even has a greed for the smallest material gain and is dishonest in the acquisition of that too, [3] The individual who spends their mornings and evenings betraying others in regard to their family and wealth, [4] The individual who is miserly and a liar, [5] The individual who habitually abuses others and uses rude and obscene language against them'.[351]

This detailed Prophetic narration highlights those individuals who are described as the inhabitants of Paradise and those described as the inhabitants of the Hellfire; each person should make every effort to implement such characteristics and to demonstrate such dealings with others that they become from the three types of

---

[349] Subul as-Salam by as-San'ani, vol 4 page 152.

[350] Sahih al-Bukhari, Hadeeth number 13.

[351] Saheeh Muslim, Hadeeth number 7386.

people mentioned to be from the people of Paradise, one should also befriend and draw close to those who will assist them in their path to becoming from the people of Paradise, for, an individual is truly influenced by the friends they keep.

خَيْرُ الْجِيرَانِ عِنْدَ اللَّهِ خَيْرُهُمْ لِجَارِهِ

The best neighbours in the sight of Allah is the best of them towards their neighbour

(Sunan at-Tirmidhi)

The Prophet ﷺ significantly emphasised the importance of neighbours, irrespective of their faith, culture and gender. The value of a neighbour can be gauged from the advice given to the Prophet ﷺ by the Angel Jibraeel, the Angel Jibraeel would advise regarding the rights of the neighbour to such an extent that the Prophet ﷺ started thinking that the Angel Jibraeel would order him to make them a part of his heirs (and hence inherit from him)'.[352]

The commentator, al-Baji RA mentions, 'It is compulsory upon every individual who believes in Allah, the rewards and the punishment of the hereafter that they show goodness towards their neighbours'.[353] The Prophet ﷺ has mentioned that honouring the neighbour and treating them well is a sign of faith, one who does not show kindness to their neighbour lacks a (major) part of faith.[354]

Imam adh-Dhahabi RA indicates to a number of essential etiquettes pertaining to the neighbour, he presents it in his compilation related to the rights of the neighbour:

[1] One should honour and show respect to their neighbour,

[2] One should behave amicably towards their neighbours (by sending gifts, doing favours for them and assisting them in moments of hardship),

[3] One should prevent (all forms of) harm that may affect the neighbour,

[4] To never gaze with the eye of immorality at the spouse of the neighbour (not only is it a major sin, but it is also a major violation of the trust and honour of the neighbour),

[5] To feed the neighbours (specifically when a special dish has been prepared or the neighbours can smell the food being cooked),

---

[352] Sahih al-Bukhari, Hadeeth number 6015.
[353] Al-Muntaqa' by al-Baji, vol 4 page 334.
[354] Sahih al-Bukhari, Hadeeth number 6018.

[6] If one is selling their house, they should consult with the neighbours first and enquire if they are interested in buying at the intended sale price, (one should even consult with the neighbours when selling to a third party, as the neighbours will have to live with and bear the brunt of the new neighbour),

[7] If one is satiated at night time before going to sleep, yet their neighbour is hungry (and doesn't have the means for food), then they are not complete believers,

[8] One should be generous to their neighbours and show kindness to them.[355]

The son of the first caliph, 'Abd ar-Rahman ﷺ (the son of Abu Bakr ﷺ) was once involved in a dispute with his neighbour, Abu Bakr ﷺ gave him a simple piece of advice, 'Do not involve yourself in any dispute with your neighbour, all other people you dispute with will go away, however, your neighbour will always remain next to you'.[356]

Imam al-Gazzaali RA has mentioned an incident of a man who complained regarding the excessive mice in his home. He was advised to keep a cat so that the mice would run away out of fear of the cat. However, the individual refused to do this and he explained, 'How can I allow myself to become from amongst those people who desire for their neighbours that which they do not desire for themselves (because the mice would leave his home and inhabit the homes of his neighbours)?"[357]

These such incidents clearly present to us the scrupulousness and attention of the pious in regard to their neighbours and the immense efforts they went to so as not to give them any harm.

---

[355] Haqq al-Jaar by Imam ad-Dhahabi. Small booklet.
[356] Ihya 'Ulum ad-Din, vol 2 page 57.
[357] Ihya 'Ulum ad-Din, vol 2 page 56.

كَانَ النَّبِيُّ صَلَّى اللهُ عَلَيْهِ وَسَلَّمَ إِذَا مَشَى كَأَنَّهُ يَتَوَكَّأُ

The Prophet ﷺ would walk leaning forward a little (with humility)

(Sunan Abu Dawood)

Almighty Allah has not only preserved the statements of the Prophet ﷺ, but He has also preserved the characteristics and features of the Prophet ﷺ and they have been meticulously captured for us by his companions, may Allah be pleased with them all and reward them immensely.

By way of example, from amongst the many characteristics is the walk of the Prophet ﷺ. Abu Hurairah ﷺ mentions, 'I have not seen anybody more handsome than the Prophet ﷺ, it is as though the brightness of the sun shone from his face. Furthermore, I did not see anyone walk at a faster pace than the Prophet ﷺ, it was as though the earth folded itself for him. We found it difficult to keep up with his pace (due to his naturally purposeful stride), yet, he was only walking at his normal pace.[358]

Shihab ad-Din ibn Hajar al-Haytami RA mentions, 'The Prophet ﷺ would not alter his walk from his natural pace, his pace was perfect (and purposeful)'.[359]

'Ali ﷺ mentions, 'The Prophet ﷺ would firmly lift his leg from the earth (he would not drag his feet along the ground), it was as though he was descending from a higher piece of earth (due to his brisk and humbled walk)'.[360]

Imam Suyuti RA mentions, 'The Prophet ﷺ would walk at a moderate pace, it was neither similar to a slumped person nor like a bounding person, he would be moderate in pace inclined towards fast, however, it was not running; rather his walking came naturally to the Prophet ﷺ and he appeared very calm'.[361]

Hafidh ibn al-Qayyim RA mentions, 'The Prophet ﷺ would walk leaning a little forward, he walked at a fast pace and was extremely calm... the walk of the Prophet ﷺ was similar to that of a brave and powerful man, a walk that was moderate and most natural to the body. He would not walk recklessly, in a slow and lazy manner, nor did the Prophet walk with uneasiness and hastily like that of a camel; rather he

---

[358] As-Shamail al-Muhammadiyyah by Imam at-Tirmidhi, Hadeeth number 125.
[359] Ashraf al-Wasil Ila' fahm al-Wasail, page 189.
[360] As-Shamail al-Muhammadiyyah by Imam at-Tirmidhi, Hadeeth number 126, 127.
[361] As-Shamail as-Shareefah by Imam As-Suyuti, page 197.

would avoid constantly turning towards the right and the left, he would look down and walk calmly, softly and with composure'.[362]

Hafidh ibn al-Qayyim RA divides the different types of walking into ten categories:

[1] A sluggish and lethargic walker, [2] A moderate and composed walker, [3] An erratic and irregular walker, [4] A fast walker inclined towards running, [5] A fast walker inclined towards jogging, [6] A wild and uncultured running pace, [7] Walking with a heavy foot, [8] An individual who walks backwards, [9] Walking with a bounce in the step, [10] Strolling with swagger and pride in the step.

He then mentions that the most appropriate from these ten is the moderately nuanced walk in a humble manner.[363] This pace is free from erratic movements and is extremely natural and dignified, this was the walk of the Prophet ﷺ.

---

[362] Za'd al-Mu'aad by Ibn al-Qayyim, vol 1 page 161.
[363] Za'd al-Mu'aad by Ibn al-Qayyim, vol 1 page 161.

مَا مِنْ شَيْءٍ أَثْقَلُ فِيْ الْمِيْزَانِ مِنْ حُسْنِ الْخُلُقِ

There is nothing heavier in the scale of the believer on the Day of Judgement than good character

(Sunan Abu Dawood)

The Prophet ﷺ once asked the Companions, 'Do you know which deeds will make a person enter Paradise the most?" He ﷺ then answered himself, "Indeed, fearing Allah (by abandoning sins and by following his commands), and good manners." He ﷺ then asked, "Do you know which deeds will make a person enter Hellfire the most?" He ﷺ again answered himself, "The mouth (i.e. not controlling the mouth) and the private parts (i.e. coming adultery)."

Mulla 'Ali al-Qari RA mentions, 'The God-fearing individual is the one who adopts good conduct with Allah, and that is achieved by following His commands, and good manners refers to the good treatment towards all of the creation. If an individual adopts these two (fulfilling the rights of Allah and His creation), then (they should be aware that) it is from the major causes of entering Paradise'.[364]

Scholars gave an immense amount of importance to the implementation of good manners, the great scholar, 'Abdullah ibn al-Mubarak رحمه الله mentioned, 'We are much more in need of a small amount of manners than we are in need of a large amount of knowledge'.[365]

The saint, Yahya ibn Muadh RA mentioned, 'Whoever adopts the good etiquette (promoted) by Almighty Allah, then that individual will truly become from amongst those beloved by Almighty Allah'.[366]

The great saint, Hasan al-Basri RA was asked to define 'good manners' and 'Islamic etiquette' in such a way that it would be conducive to gaining benefit in both worlds, he replied by indicating towards three deeds, '[1] Gaining the true understanding of religion, [2] Abstinence from the world, [3] Recognising that which is necessary upon an individual to (always remain in the obedience of) Almighty Allah'.[367]

---

[364] Mirqaat al-Mafateeh, vol 7 page 3036.
[365] Madarij as-Salikeen, vol 2 page 376.
[366] Ar-Risalah al-Qushayriyyah, page 129
[367] Ar-Risalah al-Qushayriyyah, page 129

The saint, Junaid al-Baghdadi RA mentioned to Abu Hafs RA that his etiquette with the public was very similar to the etiquette of how one would normally deal with the kings. Abu Hafs RA replied, ‘Indeed, maintaining good manners with the general public is a genuine sign of an individual’s having goodness in the heart. Furthermore, reverence to Almighty Allah is to always sit in an upright and respectable manner (this was due to his high level of God-consciousness), an individual should exert their exoteric and esoteric worship in the glorification and praise of Almighty Allah in exactly the same way an individual would sit before a king in this world’.[368]

Unfortunately, the number of individuals who exhibit pure Islamic etiquette has deteriorated, this sentiment was echoed in the words of the great scholar ‘Abdullah ibn al-Mubarak ﵀, ‘I went to seek knowledge and I attained a portion of it, however, when I went to search for etiquette and good manners, I realised that the people with good manners had perished’.[369] These, and similar such statements, should encourage us to strive in the pursuit of learning the manners and the etiquette of the scholars of the past and the great Companions of the Prophet ﷺ. It is through the reading and studying of their lifestyles that we can attempt to revive these lofty and noble manners back into our own lives and the society at large.

[368] Madarij as-Salikeen, vol 2 page 377.
[369] Gidha al-Albab Sharh Mandhumat al-Adab by Muhammad ibn Ahmad al-Hanbali, vol 1 page 27.

خَيْرُكُمْ مَنْ تَعَلَّمَ الْقُرْآنَ وَعَلَّمَهُ

The best amongst you is the one who learns the Qur'an and teaches it

(Sahih al-Bukhari)

Reciting, understanding and practicing upon the Qur'an is from amongst the major characteristics of a true and complete believer; for indeed the Qur'an contains the words of Almighty Allah. The Prophet Ibrahim عليه السلام once made a supplication to Almighty Allah, 'Oh Lord, raise amongst them (the people) a messenger who recites unto them Your verses, teaches them the Book and the wisdom, and he cleanses them of all (physical and spiritual) impurities'.[370] In this verse, the Prophet Ibrahim عليه السلام supplicated to Almighty Allah for a messenger who would recite the verses of Allah and also teach them to mankind. Indeed learning and teaching the Qur'an is a Prophetic trait.

This has been reiterated by the Prophet ﷺ in the words, 'The best amongst you is the one who learns the Qur'an and teaches it'.[371] The learning and teaching of the Qur'an includes not only the gaining of proficiency in the actual recitation of the Qur'an, but it also includes learning and understanding the messages and advices of the Qur'an too. This is a recurrent theme found in the scholars of the past wherein they would demonstrate immense zeal and priority towards the understanding of the Qur'an.

The scholar, Abu Bakr Muhammad ibn al-Husayn RA mentioned, 'Delivering lessons on smaller portions of the Qur'an with a deeper level of understanding is much more preferred to myself than the reading of many parts of the Qur'an which is devoid of depth, understanding and contemplation, the Qur'an itself indicates upon this notion, as do the Prophetic narrations and the sayings of the pious scholars too'.[372]

Another etiquette of the Qur'an is that we should not study or teach the Qur'an with the primary motive of gaining worldly riches; rather, the primary motivation for studying and teaching the Qur'an should be for seeking the eternal pleasure of Almighty Allah. The scholar, Zadhan RA mentions, 'Whoever reads the Qur'an so that he can eat from the (charity of the) people, he will be brought forth on the day

---

[370] Surah al-Baqarah, surah 2 verse 129.

[371] Sahih al-Bukhari, Hadeeth number 5027.

[372] Akhlaaq ahl-Qur'an, page 169.

of Judgment in such a manner that his face will be mere bones which are devoid of any flesh'.[373]

Another etiquette of the Qur'an is to recite it with a beautiful voice, the scholar Abu Bakr Muhammad ibn al-Husayn RA mentioned, 'An individual who has been bestowed with a beautiful voice should know that Almighty Allah has favoured them with loftiness, they should appreciate this favour and oft recite the Qur'an for the pleasure of Almighty Allah and not recite it ostentatiously for the creation (for show). One should definitely avoid reciting the Qur'an to others merely to receive praise and a higher status in this meagre world... if one uses their beautiful voice for gaining the worldly benefits, then I fear this voice is a trial and a test for them; indeed, the beautiful voice only benefits those who have consciousness of Almighty Allah at all times'.[374]

The scholars would place immense value to the people of the Qur'an and would believe that the Qur'an is a solution for many evils and vices within the world. Maymun ibn Mahran RA would say, 'If the people of the Qur'an (i.e. the people given the knowledge of the Qur'an and have a special bond with the Qur'an) are upright, then the remaining people will also become upright.[375]

Many other etiquettes have also been mentioned by scholars in regard to the Qur'an, however, one of the most important etiquettes of the Qur'an is to implement the injunctions therein. The Prophet ﷺ mentioned 'Allah elevates (the status of) some by means of this book and He degrades others (by means of the very same book)'.[376] For, only those who value and practice upon the book will be truly elevated by Almighty Allah; whereas, those who reject the book will be degraded by Almighty Allah, whether in this temporal world or ultimately in the eternal hereafter.

[373] Akhlaaq ahl-Qur'an, page 129.
[374] Akhlaaq ahl-Qur'an, page 158.
[375] Akhlaaq ahl-Qur'an, page 104.
[376] Sahih Muslim, Hadeeth number 1934.

Bibliography

Abu al-'Abbas al-Qurtubi, Ahmad ibn 'Umar ibn Ibrahim. 1996. *al-Mufhim, Sharh Saheeh Muslim.* First. Damascus: Dar Ibn Katheer .

Abu al-'Ala al-Mubarakpuri, Muhammad 'Abdurrahman ibn 'Abdurraheem. n.d. *Tuhfah al-Ahwadhi, Sharh Sunan at-Tirmidhi.* Beirut : Dar al-Kutub al-'Ilmiyyah.

Abu al-Hasan Ibn Battal, 'Ali ibn Khalaf. 2003. *Sharh ibn Battal ala Saheeh al-Bukhari.* Second. Riyadh: Maktabah ar-Rushd.

Abu al-Waleed al-Baji, Sulayman ibn Kalaf ibn Sa'd. n.d. *al-Muntaqa'.*

Abu Dawood, Sulayman ibn al-Ash'ath as-Sijistani. 2009. *Sunan Abu Dawood.* First. Beirut: Dar ar-Risalah al-'Alamiyyah.

Abu Hayyan al-Andalusi, Muhammad ibn Yusuf. 1999. *al-Bahr al-Muheet, Tafseer.* Beirut: Dar al-Fikr.

Abu 'Isa at-Tirmidhi, Muhammad ibn 'Isa ibn Sawrah. n.d. *as-Shamail al-Muhammadiyyah.* Beirut: Mussasah al-Kutub.

—. 2014. *Sunan at-Tirmidhi.* First. Cairo: Dar at-Taaseel.

Abu Nu'aym al-Asbahani, Ahmad ibn 'Abdullah. 1985. *Hilyah al-Awliya'.* Fourth. Beirut : Dar al-Kitab al-'Arabi.

ad-Dhahabi, Shams ad-Din Abu 'Abdullah Muhammad ibn Ahmad. 1985. *Haqq al-Jaar.* Dar 'Alaam.

—. n.d. *Siyar 'Alam an-Nubala'.* Mu'assasah ar-Risalah .

—. 1987. *Tareekh al-Islam.* First. Beirut: Dar al-Kitab al-'Arabi.

Ahmad ibn Hanbal, Ahmad ibn Muhammad ibn Hanbal. n.d. *az-Zuhd.* Beirut: Dar al-Kutub al-'ilmiyyah.

Ahmad ibn Hanbal, Ahmad ibn Muhammad. 2001. *Musnad Ahmad ibn Hanbal.* First. Beirut: Muassasah ar-Risalah.

al-Aajurri, Muhammad Abu Bakr ibn al-Husayn. 2003. *Akhlaaq ahl-Qur'an.* Thrid. Beirut: Dar al-Kutub al-'Ilmiyyah.

al-Alusi, Shihab ad-Din Mahmud ibn 'Abdullah. 1995. *Ruh al-Ma'ni.* Beirut: Dar al-Kutub al-'Ilmiyyah.

al-Ameer as-San'ani, Muhammad ibn Isma'il ibn Salah. 2011. *at-Tanweer, Sharh al-Jami' as-Sagheer.* First. Riyadh: Maktabah Dar as-Salam.

al-'Ayni, Badr ad-Din. 2006. *'Umdah al-Qari.* Second.

al-'Azeem al-Aabadi, Abu at-Tayyib Muhammad Shams al-Haqq. 1968. *'Awn al-Ma'bood, Sharh Sunan Abu Dawood.* Second. Madinah: al-Maktabah as-Salafiyyah.

al-Bagawi, al-Husayn ibn Mas'ud. 1983. *Sharh as-Sunnah.* Second. Damascus, Beirut: al-Maktab al-Islami.

al-Bayhaqi, Ahmad ibn al-Husayn ibn 'Ali ibn Musa. 2003. *Shu'ab al-Iman.* First. Riyadh: Maktabah ar-Rushd.

al-Birmawi, Shams ad-Din Abu 'Abdullah Muhammad ibn 'Abd ad-Da'im ibn Musa. 2012. *al-Lami' as-Sabeeh* . First. Syria: Dar an-Nawadir.

al-Bukhari, Muhammad ibn Isma'il. 1989. *Al-Adab al-Mufrad.* Third. Beirut: Dar al-Bashair al-Islamiyyah.

—. 1987. *Saheeh al-Bukhari.* First. Cairo: Dar as-Sa'b.

al-Gazzali, Muhammad ibn Muhammad. n.d. *Ihya 'Ulum ad-Din.*

al-Harari, Muhammad al-Amin ibn 'Abdullah. 2009. *al-Kawkab al-Wahhaj.* First. Dar al-Minhaj.

al-Haytami, Aḥmad ibn Muhammad ibn Hajar. 1998. *Ashraf al-Wasil Ila' fahm al-Wasail.* First. Beirut : Dar al-Kutub al-'Ilmiyyah .

'Ali ibn Abu Talib. n.d. *Diwan 'Ali ibn Abu Talib.*

al-Jurjani, 'Ali ibn Muhammad ibn 'Ali. 1985. *at-Ta'reefat.* First. Beirut : Dar al-Kitab al-'Arabi.

al-Kharaiti, Abu Bakr Muhammad ibn Ja'far ibn Sahl. n.d. *Masawi' al-Akhlaaq.*

al-Khattabi, Abu Sulayman Ahmad ibn Muhammad. 1932. *Ma'lim as-Sunan.* First. Halab: al-Matba'ah al-'Ilmiyyah .

al-Khazin, Tafseer. 1995. *al-Khazin, 'Ala ad-Din ibn Muhammad ibn Ibraheem al-Baghdadi.* Beirut: Dar al-Kutub al-'Ilmiyyah.

al-Kurani, Ahmad ibn Isma'il ibn 'Uthman ibn Muhammad. 2008. *al-Kawthar al-Jari.* First. Beirut : Dar Ihya at-Turath al-'Arabi.

al-Maghribi al-La'ee, al-Husayn ibn Muhammad ibn Sa'eed. 2007. *alBadr at-Tamaam Sharh Bulugh al-Maram* . First. Dar Hijr.

al-Maqdisi, Ibn Qudamah. 1978. *Mukhtasar Minhaj al-Qasideen.* Damascus : Maktabah Dar al-Bayan.

al-Mawardi, Abu al-Hasan 'Ali ibn Muhammad ibn Muhammad ibn Habeeb al-Basri. n.d. *an-Nukat wal-'Uyoon, Tafseer al-Mawardi.* Beirut : Dar al-Kutub al-'Ilmiyyah.

al-Mawardi, 'Ali ibn Muhammad ibn Habib al-Mawardi as-Shafe'e. n.d. *Adab ad-Dunya' Wad-Din* .

al-Munawi, Zayn ad-Din Muhammad 'Abd ar-Ra'uf ibn Taj al-'Arifeen ibn 'Ali. 1988. *at-Tayseer Bi-Sharh al-Jami' as-Sagheer.* Third. Riyadh: Maktabah al-Imam as-Shafe'e.

—. 1994. *Faydh al-Qadeer.* First. Beirut: Dar al-Kutub al-'Ilmiyyah.

al-Mundhiri, Abu Muhammad 'Abdulazeem ibn 'Abdulqawiy. 1997. *at-Targheeb wat-Tarheeb.* First. Beirut : Dar al-Kutub al-'Ilmiyyah.

al-Muzhiri, al-Husayn ibn Mahmood ibn al-Hasan az-Zaydani. 2012. *al-Mafatih* . First. Dar an-Nawadir.

al-Qadhi al-Baydhawi, Nasir ad-Din 'Abdullah ibn 'Umar. 2012. *Tuhfah al-Abraar, Sharh Miskhaat* . Kuwait: Wizarah al-Awqaaf Kuwait.

al-Qadhi 'Iyadh, 'Iyadh ibn Musa ibn 'Iyadh ibn 'Imran. 1998. *Ikmaal al-Mu'lim, Sharh Saheeh Muslim.* First. Egypt: Dar al-Wafa.

al-Qadi Ibn al-'Arabi, Muhammad ibn 'Abdullah. 2003. *Ahkaam al-Qur'an.* Third. Lebanon: Dar al-Kutub al-'Ilmiyyah .

al-Qari, 'Ali ibn Sultan. n.d. *Jam' al-Wasail.* Egypt: al-Matba'ah as-Sharfiyyah.

—. 2002. *Mirqaat al-Mafateeh.* First. Beirut: Dar al-Fikr.

al-Qastallani, Ahmad ibn Muhammad ibn Abu Bakr. n.d. *Irshad as-Sari* . Seventh. Egypt: al-Matba'h al-Kubra.

al-Qurtubi, Muhammad Abu 'Abdullah ibn Ahmad. 2003. *Tafseer al-Qurtubi.* Riyadh: Dar 'Alam al-Kutub.

al-Qushayri, 'Abd al-Kareem ibn Hawazin. n.d. *ar-Risalah al-Qushayriyyah* .

al-'Ushrah, Aadab. n.d. *al-Gazzi, Badr ad-Din Abu al-Barakaat Muhammad ibn Muhammad* .

an-Nasai, Abu 'Abdurrahman Ahmad ibn Shu'ayb. 1406. *al-Mujtaba, Sunan an-Nasai.* Halab: Maktabah al-Matbu'at al-Islamiyyah.

an-Nawawi, Abu Zakariyya Yahya ibn Sharaf. n.d. *Bustan al-'Arifeen.*

an-Nawawi, Abu Zakriyya Yahya ibn Sharaf. 1972. *al-Minhaj, Sharh Saheeh Muslim.* Second. Beirut : Dar Ihya at-Turath.

as-Safarini, Muhammad ibn Ahmad ibn Salim al-Hanbali. 2002. *Gidha al-Albab Sharh Mandhumat al-Adab.* Second. Beirut: Dar al-Kutub al-'Ilmiyyah.

as-Sama'ni, Abu al-Muzaffar Mansur ibn Muhammad ibn 'Abdul Jabbar. 1997. *Taseer as-Sama'ni.* Riyadh: Dar al-Watan.

as-Sana'ni, Abu Bakr 'Abd ar-Razzaq ibn Hammam ibn Nafi'. 1983. *Musannaf 'Abd ar-Razzaq.* Second. Beirut : al-Majlis al-'Ilmi.

as-San'ani, Muhammad ibn Isma'el al-Ameer. 1960. *Subul as-Salam* . Fourth . Maktabah Mustafah al-Babi.

as-Sindi, Muhammad ibn 'Abdul Hadi. n.d. *Hashiyah ala Sunan an-Nasai.*

—. n.d. *Hashiyah 'Ala Sunan Ibn Majah.*

—. n.d. *Hashiyah as-Sindi 'Ala Saheeh al-Bukhari.* Dar al-Fikr.

as-Sulami, Abu 'Abdurrahman Muhammad ibn al-Husayn ibn Musa al-Azdi. 2001. *Tafseer as-Sulami.* Beirut : Dar al-Kutub al-'Ilmiyyah .

as-Suyuti, Jalal ad-Din 'Abd ar-Rahman. n.d. *ad-Dibaaj 'Ala Muslim.*

—. 2003. *ad-Durr al-Manthur, Tafseer as-Suyuti.* Egypt: Dar Hijr.

—. n.d. *as-Shamail as-Shareefah* . Dar Ta'ir al-'Ilm .

—. n.d. *Hashiyah ala Sunan an-Nasai.*

at-Tabrani, Abul Qasim Sulayman ibn Ahmad ibn Ayyub. 1995. *al-Mu'jam al-Awsat.* Cairo: Dar al-Haramain.

—. n.d. *al-Mu'jam al-Kabeer.*

at-Teebi, al-Husayn ibn 'Abdullah. 1997. *al-Kashif 'An Haqaiq as-Sunan.* First. Riyadh: Maktabah Nizaar.

at-Turibishti, Fadlullah ibn Hasan ibn Husayn. 2008. *al-Muyassar* . Second. Maktabah Nizaar .

az-Zuhayli, Doctor Wahbah ibn Mustafah. 2001. *at-Tafseer al-Waseet* . First. Damascus : Dar al-Fikr.

az-Zurqani, Muhammad ibn 'Abdul Baqi ibn Yusuf. 1991. *Sharh az-Zurqani 'Ala Muwatta.* Beirut : Dar al-Kutub al-'Ilmiyyah.

Fakr ad-Din ar-Razi, Muhammad ibn 'Umar. n.d. *Mafateeh al-Ghayb, Tafseer ar-Razi.* Beirut : Dar Ihya at-Turath.

Ibn 'Aashoor, Muhammad at-Tahir ibn Muhammad. 2000. *at-Tahreer wat-Tanweer, Tafseer Ibn 'Aashoor* . First . Beirut : Muassasah at-Tarikh al-'Arabi.

Ibn 'Abd al-Barr. n.d. *al-Idhtidhkaar.*

Ibn 'Abd al-Barr, Abu 'Umar Yusuf ibn 'Abdullah ibn Muhammad. n.d. *at-Tamheed* . Muassisah al-Qurtubah .

Ibn Abi ad-Dunya, 'Abdullah ibn Muhammad al-Qurashi. 1988. *al-Ikhwaan.* First. Beirut: Dar al-Kutub al-'Ilmiyyah.

—. 1990. *as-Samt wa-Adaab al-Lisaan.* First. Beirut: Dar al-Kitab al-'Arabi.

—. 1989. *at-Tawadu' wal-Kumool* . First. Beirut : Dar al-Kutub al-'Ilmiyyah .

—. 1988. *Husn ad-Dhann bi-Allah.* First. Riyadh: Dar Taybah.

—. 1990. *Makarim al-Akhlaaq.* Cairo: Maktabah al-Qur'an.

Ibn Abu Hatim ar-Razi, Abu Muhammad 'Abdurrahman ibn Abu Hatim. n.d. *Tafseer Ibn Abu Hatim* . al-Maktabah al-'Asriyyah.

Ibn al-Jawzi, Jamal ad-Din Abu al-Faraj 'Abdurrahman. n.d. *Bahr ad-Dumu'.*

—. 1997. *Kashf al-Mushkil.* Riyadh: Dar an-Nashr.

—. 1979. *Sifah as-Safwah.* Second. Beirut : Dar al-Ma'rifah.

Ibn al-Malak ar-Rumi, Muhammad ibn 'Izz ad-Din al-Kirmani al-Hanafi. 2012. *Sharh Masabih as-Sunnah.* First. Idarah at-Tiqafah al-Islamiyyah.

Ibn al-Mulaqqin, Siraj ad-Din 'Umar ibn 'Ali ibn Ahmad. 2008. *at-Tawdheeh, Sharh Sahih al-Bukhari.* First. Damascus : Dar an-Nawadir.

Ibn as-Sariyy, Hannad. 1986. *az-Zuhd.* Kuwait: Dar al-Kulafa'.

Ibn Daqeeq al-'Eed, Taqi ad-Din Abul Fath Muhammad ibn 'Ali al-Qushayri. 2005. *Ihkam al-Ahkam, Sharh 'Umdah al-Ahkam.* First. Mussasah ar-Risalah.

ibn Hajar al-'Asqalani, Ahmad ibn 'Ali. n.d. *Fath al-Bari.* Beirut: Dar al-Ma'rifah.

Ibn Hajar al-Haytami, Ahmad ibn Muhammad al-Makki. n.d. *az-Zawajir 'An Iqtiraf al-Kabair.*

Ibn Hubayrah, 'Awn ad-Din Abu al-Muzaffar Yahya ibn Hubayrah ibn Muhammad. 1997. *Al-Ifsah 'An M'ani as-Sihah.* Dar al-Watan.

Ibn Jareer at-Tabari, Abu Ja'far Muhammad ibn Jareer ibn Yazeed. 2000. *Tafseer at-Tabari.* First. Mussasat ar-Risalah.

Ibn Jizzi, Muhammad ibn Ahmad al-Garnati al-Maliki. n.d. *at-Tasheel li 'Ulum at-Tanzeel* .

Ibn Katheer, Isma'el Abul Fida' ibn 'Umar. 1999. *Tafseer Ibn Katheer.* Second. Dar Taybah.

Ibn Majah al-Qazweeni, Muhammad ibn Yazeed. 2009. *Sunan Ibn Majah.* First. Beirut: Dar ar-Risalah al-'Alamiyyah.

Ibn Muflih, Muhammad Abu 'Abdullah al-Maqdisi. n.d. *al-Adab as-Shar'iyyah.*

Ibn Qayyim al-Jawziyyah, Muhammad ibn Abu Bakr. 1973. *al-Fawaid.* Second. Beirut : Dar al-Kutub al-'Ilmiyyah.

—. 1997. *al-Jawab al-Kafi.* Dar al-Ma'rifah.

—. 1975. *Igaathah al-Lahfaan.* Second. Beirut: Dar al-Ma'rifah.

—. 1987. *Jila' al-Afhaam* . Second. Kuwait: Dar al-'Arubah.

—. 1973. *Madarij as-Salikeen.* Second. Beirut: Dar al-Kitab al-'Arabi.

—. n.d. *Miftah Dar as-Sa'dah.* Beirut: Dar al-Kutub al-'Ilmiyyah.

—. 1989. *'Uddah as-Sabireen .* Third. Madinah: Dar at-Turath.

—. n.d. *Zaad al-Ma'aad.*

Ibn Qutaybah, Abu Muhammad 'Abdullah ibn Muslim. 1977. *Ghareeb al-Hadeeth.* First. Baghdad: Matba'ah al-'Aani.

Ibn Rajab al-Hanbali, Abu al-Faraj 'Abdurrahman ibn Ahmad. 1979. *at-Takweef min an-Nar.* First. Damascus : Maktabah Dar al-Bayan.

—. 2001. *Fath al-Bari.* Second. Dammam: Dar ibn al-Jawzi.

—. n.d. *Ikhtiyaar al-Uwla fi Sharh Hadeeth Iktisaam al-Mala' al-A'la.*

—. 1988. *Jami' al-'Ulum wal-Hikam.* First. Beirut : Dar al-Ma'rifah.

Ibn Taymiyyah al-Harrani, Taqi ad-Din Abul 'Abbas Ahmad ibn 'Abd al-Haleem. 2005. *Majmu' al-Fatawa.* Third. Dar al-Wafa.

ibn-'Allan, Muhammad 'Ali ibn Muhammad. n.d. *Daleel al-Faliheen.*

Jamal ad-Din al-Qasmi, Muhammad ibn Muhammad Sa'eed ibn Qasim. 1995. *Maw'idhah al-Mumineen .* Beirut : Dar al-Kutub al-'Ilmiyyah.

Lasheen, Ustadh Musa Saheen. 2002. *Fath al-Mun'im .* First. Dar as-Shurooq.

Makki ibn Abu Talib, Abu Muhammad Makki ibn Abu Talib Hammoosh ibn Muhammad. 2008. *al-Hidayah Ila buloogh an-Nihayah.* Jami' as-Sharooqah .

Muhammad as-Shanqitee, Muhammad al-Kadhir ibn 'Abdullah ibn Ahmad. 1995. *Kawthar al-Mani' ad-Darari, Sharh Saheeh al-Bukhari.* First. Beirut : Mussasah ar-Risalah.

Muslim an-Naysaburi, Abu al-Husayn ibn al-Hajjaj al-Qushairi. n.d. *Saheeh Muslim.* Beirut: Dar al-Jeel.

Usmani, Muhammad Taqi. 2014. *In'am al-Bari.* Karachi: Maktaba hera.

Our publications

Jamiatul Ilm Wal Huda

1000 Hadith for Memorisation (in Arabic with English translation)

This book is a compilation of a 1000 authentic narrations of Prophet Muhammad ﷺ from the six famous books, it is designed in chapter form. The book has originally been created for memorisation, yet it can be useful for general reading as well. The 1000 narrations have been translated into easy flowing English, easily understandable for all. A book that would not only be of great benefit in the classroom environment, rather it will be very useful for study circles and daily reminders at home as well. In sha Allah.

Usool al-Hadith (in Arabic)

This book is aimed at teaching Usool al-Hadith to an intermediate level; in an easy format. It is filled with tables and flowcharts; this style has been adopted to make the subject as easy as possible to understand. Furthermore, flowcharts have been added at the end of the book which covers majority of the subject.

Mantiq (in Arabic)

This book is aimed at teaching the classical Mantiq (logic) terms to an intermediate level; in an easy format. It is filled with tables and flowcharts; this style has been adopted to make the subject as easy as possible to understand. Furthermore, flowcharts have been added at the end of the book which covers majority of the subject.

Zahratun Nahw (part 1)

This book is designed for teaching Nahw (Arabic syntax) for the beginner level. It has adopted a very simple style with very simple terms indicated. The depth of the subject has been avoided; aiming to consolidate the very basics of grammar for the learners.

Hidayatun Nahw (with Q&A in English)

The book Hidayatun Nahw is a book taught in many places for intermediate level Nahw. However, due to its complex text, many readers find many parts of the text difficult to solve. Therefore, for the English speaking readers, this book was designed with the intention of making the complex text of the book easier for understanding. Hence, the English question & answers do not go into much detail beyond the content of the book; it is more based on solving the book.

Qisas an-Nabiyeen (part 1-4)

Qisas an-Nabiyyeen is a compilation of short and entertaining stories about some of the Messengers. It was written by Shaykh Abul Hasan Ali an-Nadwi for students starting to learn the Arabic language. The Jamiatul Ilm Wal Huda publication has the original text with an addition of over 2500 words of Arabic vocabulary with English and Urdu meanings.

Qisas an-Nabiyeen (part 5)

Qisas an-Nabiyyeen is a compilation of short and entertaining stories about some of the Messengers, part 5 is dedicated to the final Prophet, Muhammad. It was written by Shaykh Abul Hasan Ali an-Nadwi for students starting to learn the Arabic language. The Jamiatul Ilm Wal Huda publication has the original text with an addition of over 1300 words of Arabic vocabulary with English and Urdu meanings. Further, this publication has added footnotes of certain names and events and added additional Seerah information at the end of the book.

Das Sabak (in Urdu & English)

The book Das Sabak is a book taught in many institutes as a beginners guide for Arabic learning. The book covers ten very important topics of Arabic grammar; allowing the students to become equipped with the foundation before enhancing to intermediate level. The book was designed to make translation of the Qur'an easier for beginners; covering most words up to half of the first para. However, as the book was written in Urdu, it became hard for the English speaking audience to take benefit from the book; hence, the need arose to make a parallel English version of the book. The Urdu has been kept within the book, with explanatory English notes for each chapter.

A Comprehensive Guide To Tajweed

This book is aimed at teaching enhanced level Tajweed according to the recitation of Imam Hafs. Many simple books have been written in the English language on the subject of Tajweed; however, most were restricted to the beginner's level. Hence, the need arose to compile a book of advanced level which would enable the English speaking audience to learn detailed Tajweed directly from an English source. This book will allow the reader to straight away solve many of the detailed books of Tajweed within the Arabic language. It may even prove to be a commentary for many of the Arabic texts.

Training the Students of Sacred Knowledge (in English)

This book is aimed at teaching the students of the sacred knowledge the etiquettes of studying. This book *Riyāḍat al-Muta'allīmīn* is indispensable and beneficial especially for students of knowledge and teachers. Imam Ibn al-Sunnī outlines the etiquettes and guidelines for students and teachers, the methods of teaching and learning, and the different sciences that should be acquired. This compilation has translated the original work in a reader friendly manner, mentioning the approximately 300 etiquettes with proofs from narrations.

Durus al-Lughah al-Arabiyyah (part 1)

Durus al-lughah al-Arabiyyah is a book taught in many institutes as a beginners/intermediate guide for Arabic learning. Book 1 covers 23 important chapters of Arabic grammar, language and literature; allowing the students to become equipped with the foundation/intermediate before enhancing to higher level. The book was designed specifically for non-Arab students intending to learn basic writing, reading and speaking skills within modern-day Arabic. This publication explains the core lessons and meanings of each chapter in English, along with additional notes at the end of important modern-day Arabic words not covered within the original book.

Durus al-Lughah al-Arabiyyah (part 2)

Durus al-lughah al-Arabiyyah is a book taught in many institutes as a beginners/intermediate guide for Arabic learning. Book 2 covers 31 important chapters of Arabic grammar, language and literature; allowing the students to become equipped with the foundation/intermediate before enhancing to higher level. The book was designed specifically for non-Arab students intending to learn basic writing, reading and speaking skills within modern-day Arabic. This publication explains the core lessons and meanings of each chapter in English, along with additional notes at the end of important modern-day Arabic words not covered within the original book.

Al-Muqaddimah al-Jazariyyah

Al-Muqaddimah al-Jazariyyah is a compilation of tajweed rules by Shams al-Din al-Jazari in over 100 poems. The Jamiatul Ilm Wal Huda publication has the original text with an addition of English translation/explanation; allowing readers to easily understand the Arabic lines.

Suwar min Hayat as-Sahabiyyaat

Suwar min Hayat as-Sahabiyyat is a compilation of short and entertaining stories about eight female Companions. It was written by Shaykh Abdul Rahman Ra'fat al-Pasha for students starting to learn the Arabic language. The Jamiatul Ilm Wal Huda publication has the original text with an addition of over 1000 words of Arabic vocabulary with English and Urdu meanings; also, a brief of each female scholar in the English language.

Diwan of Imam Shafe'e

The compilation includes the Arabic poetry of Imam Shafe'e with explanatory translation in English. A very simple and easy style of translation has been adopted, allowing all to benefit from the valuable advices and lessons captured by Imam Shafe'e within his poetry. It should hopefully serve beneficial for students of Arabic along with those that are unable to read or understand Arabic. Furthermore, there is a vocabulary list of the difficult words in footnotes allowing students to benefit further. Also, a treatise of Arabic poetry rules in English has been added to the beginning of the compilation for further benefit.

40 Hadeeth on Islamic Manners

Islam teaches us the great importance of manners and etiquettes to the extent that it has been regarded as the weightiest deed in the scale of good deeds. This compilation of 40 Hadeeth with translation and explanation of the 40 Hadeeth will, insha Allah, serve as a means of encouragement to us all; young, old, students, scholars, laity etc. The style of the explanation has been kept very simple with approximately two sides of explanation for each Hadeeth, most of the explanation are simply capturing Qur'an verses, other Prophetic narrations or sayings of the pious scholars in regards to the topic discussed. The chapters included are wide ranging, from mercy to parents, anger to jealousy, treatment towards Muslims and non-Muslims, rights of the Lord to the rights of the creation and so.

A preview of these books can be viewed by visiting the following link:

http://www.jamiah.co.uk/achievements/jamiah-publications/